DICTIONARY

Compiled by Donna Bailey
Illustrated by Pauline Banazi,
Julie Cooke, Jo Davies,
Brian Hoskins, Alan Howe,
Patti Pearce and Stephen Sweet

© 1993 Henderson Publishing Limited

Woodbridge, England

A

Headwords: 4,000 useful words are listed A to Z, These are verbs, nouns or adjectives, all in frequent use. Verbs are given in the infinitive, with past tense where it is irregular, i.e. **bring/brought.**
Definitions: Different meanings are numbered. Words which come from the headword, e.g. an adjective from a noun, are in brackets. Headwords appear in context printed in italics. Unusual pronunciation is also noted, i.e. (say boh).

abandon to give up or leave, and not come back

abbreviate to make something shorter (abbreviation)

abdomen the lower part of the body where the stomach is (abdominal)

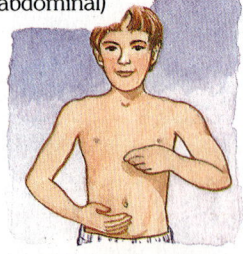

able having the skill or power to do something (ability)

abnormal not usual, strange (abnormality)

abolish to do away with or put an end to (abolition)

abroad in a foreign country

absent away from school, or at another place; not present (absence)

absorb to soak up (absorbtion)

absurd ridiculous, silly (absurdity)

abundant plentiful, in large amounts (abundance)

accelerate to go faster (accelerator, acceleration)

accent a way of speaking that sounds different

accept to take or receive (acceptance)

accident when something happens by chance (accidental)

accommodate to provide lodgings (accommodation)

accompany to go with (accompaniment)

accomplice a person who helps commit a crime

accountant a person who checks the money or accounts of a business

accurate correct and careful (accuracy)

accuse to blame for a crime (accuser, accusation)

accustom to be used to

ache a dull pain

acid a sharp sour liquid (acidity)

acorn the fruit or seed of an oak tree

acquire to get or obtain (acquisition)

acrobat a person who does somersaults and balancing tricks on wires

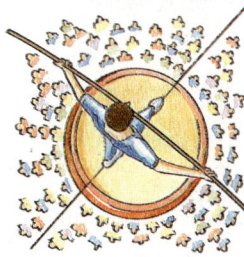

act 1. something one does, a deed (action, activity): *Peter's act of bravery saved the child's life.*
2. to behave in a certain way: *The man acted as if he had had too much to drink.*
3. to take part in a stage play (actor, actress): *John acted the part of the wizard.*

actual real

adapt to change or alter something for a different use (adaptation)

add to join together so as to form a complete whole (addition)

adder a small poisonous snake

address the name of the house, street and town where one lives

adequate just enough

adjust to make a correction (adjustment)

admiral the most important officer in a navy

admire to have a good opinion of (admirer, admiration)

admit 1. to allow somebody to enter (admission): *Nobody was admitted after the concert had begun.*
2. to confess or tell about: *Jane admitted she had broken the vase.*

adopt to agree to bring up somebody else's child as your own (adoption)

adore to love very much (adoration)

adorn to make beautiful or decorate (adornment)

DICTIONARY 3

A

adult a grown-up person

advance to move forward

advantage to have a better position or to benefit from

adventure an unusual and exciting experience

advertise to make something known to the public (advertisement)

advise to make a suggestion about what one should do (adviser, advice)

aeroplane a flying machine

afford to have enough money to buy

afraid frightened

after behind, later in time

afternoon the time between midday and evening

again once more

age 1. the number of years a person has lived: *Joe is seven years of age.* 2. a period of time: *During the Stone Age, people used stone tools.*

agent a person who acts for another (agency)

aggravate to make worse (aggravation)

agile nimble, able to move quickly and easily (agility)

agony great pain (agonizing)

agree to consent or accept (agreement)

agriculture growing crops and rearing animals (agricultural)

ahead in front, forwards

aid to help (assistance)

aim to point at, to try to reach

air the gases in the atmosphere around the Earth

airborne carried by air

aircraft carrier a large warship that carries planes and has a wide deck where they can land and take off

airport a place with long flat runways where aircraft can land and take off

airtight sealed so that no air can enter

aisle a passage between rows of seats, especially in a theatre or church

ajar slightly open

alarm 1. a warning of danger: *The thief set off the burglar alarm.* 2. to frighten: *The child was alarmed by the strange man.*

albatross a very large sea bird

album a book for storing collections of stamps or photographs

alcohol a strong colourless liquid which, in drinks, can make people drunk (alcoholic)

alert wide awake and ready to act quickly (alertness)

alibi a claim to be somewhere else when a crime was committed

alien foreign, strange

alike almost the same

alive living and breathing

all every one, the whole lot

alleviate to make less

alley a narrow passage between buildings

allow to give permission or agree to

ally a friend or friendly country in time of war

almost nearly

aloft on high, above the ground

alone on one's own

aloud in a spoken voice; not silently

alphabet the 26 letters we use to write down words

already before a certain time

also as well as

altar a raised table in a church where gifts are offered

alter to change (alteration)

alternative a choice of two things

altitude the height above sea level

aluminium a very light weight metal

always at all times

amateur a person who does not earn money from a sport or hobby

A

amaze to surprise very much (amazement)

ambition desire for success or power (ambitious)

ambulance a large van to carry sick people

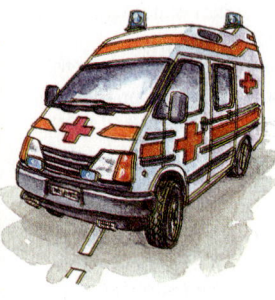

ambush a group of armed people in hiding while they wait to attack an enemy by surprise

ammunition bullets fired from guns

amount 1. to add up to a total: *The price of the tickets amounted to over £100.*
2. a total or quantity: *The dog drank a small amount of water.*

amphibious able to live on land and in water

ample plenty

amuse to entertain and make happy or cause laughter (amusement)

anaesthetic a drug which stops one feeling pain

ancestor members of the family one is descended from (ancestral)

anchor a heavy iron hook on a chain which digs into the seabed to hold a ship in position

ancient very old

angel a heavenly spirit or messenger (angelic)

anger a strong feeling of rage (angry)

angle 1. to fish with a rod and line (angler, angling)

2. the corner or point where two lines meet (the angle between the wall and the floor)

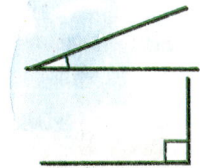

animal a living creature

ankle the joint between the foot and the lower leg

A

anniversary a day that each year celebrates something that has happened

announce to make something known to the public (announcer, announcement)

annoy to irritate or make a person cross (annoyance)

annual 1. happening every year: *We go to Spain for our annual holidays.*
2. plants which live only for one year: *Many annuals have bright petals.*
3. a book that is published once a year: *Tracy got a Christmas annual as a present.*

anonymous without a name

anorak a waterproof jacket with a hood

answer a reply to a question

ant a small insect which lives in a nest underground

antelope a kind of deer

anthem a song of praise

antique a very old object (antiquity)

antiseptic a substance that stops infection and decay

antler the horn of a male deer

anvil an iron block on which a blacksmith hammers metal objects into shape

anxious worried, uneasy (anxiety)

apart separate

ape 1. a kind of large monkey
2. to imitate or mimic: *The baby aped the behaviour of its older brother.*

apologise to say one is sorry (apology)

apparatus the tools needed for doing a job

appeal to ask very earnestly

appear 1. to come into sight (appearance): *The cat appeared around the corner of the house.*
2. to seem: *The child appeared to be perfectly healthy.*

appetite a need for food (appetizing)

applaud to clap or shout in enjoyment (applause)

apple the round firm fleshy fruit of an apple tree

DICTIONARY 7

apply 1. to ask for (application): *The man applied for a new job.* 2. to put on: *Jack applied a coat of paint to the fence.*

approach 1. to come near: *Rita approached the horse very carefully.* 2. the path or road towards a place: *The house is approached by an avenue of trees.*

approve to think well of (approval)

apricot an oval, orange-yellow fruit like a plum

April the fourth month of the year

apron a covering worn over the front of one's clothes to keep them clean or protect them

aquarium a tank which holds fish and water plants

arch a stone or brick structure built in a curve

archery shooting with bows and arrows

architect a person who designs buildings

area an open space or piece of land

argue to debate or discuss different opinions (argument)

arid very dry

arm 1. the part of the body between the shoulder and the hand 2. to supply with weapons (arms): *The king armed his troops.*

armour a metal covering to protect the body in battle

army a large group of men trained to fight in wars

around on all sides

arrange 1. to set in order (arrangement): *Mary arranged the flowers in the vase.* 2. to plan: *Ruth arranged to meet Sue that afternoon.*

arrest to stop or seize

arrive to reach somewhere (arrival)

arrow a pointed stick shot from a bow

art a human skill of making music, poetry or paintings (artist, artistic)

article 1. a piece of writing in a newspaper or magazine
2. a thing or object: *Every article in the shop was made by hand.*

artificial not natural or real

ash 1. the dry, grey dusty remains of a fire (ashen)
2. a tree with small red berries

ashamed feeling shame or discomfort for having done something wrong

ask to request or enquire

asleep at rest and not awake

assemble to build or come together (assembly)

assist to help (assistant, assistance)

asthma an illness which makes breathing difficult (asthmatic)

astonish to surprise greatly (astonishment)

astronaut a person who travels in space

athlete a person who is very good at different sports (athletic)

atlas a book of maps of the world

atmosphere the air, gases, clouds and water vapour surrounding the Earth (atmospheric)

atom a very tiny unit of matter (atomic)

atrocious wicked, horrible (atrocity)

attach to fasten or tie (attachment)

attack to go and fight against

attempt to try

attend 1. to go to, be present at (attendance): *Peter attended the meeting in the village.*
2. to be of service to: *The doctor attended his patients.*
3. to give one's mind to (attention): *The pupils paid attention to the teacher.*

attic a space under the roof of a house

DICTIONARY 9

A

attract 1. to rouse interest (attraction): *The exhibition attracted many visitors.* 2. to draw towards: *A magnet attracts iron filings.*

auction a public sale where a person who offers the highest amount of money buys the object (auctioneer)

audible able to be heard

audience the people watching a show or event

August the eight month of the year

aunt the sister of your father or mother

authentic real, genuine

author a person who writes books and articles

autograph a person's signature or own handwriting

automatic working by itself, without any help

autumn the season between summer and winter (autumnal)

avalanche a mass of snow and ice moving down the side of a mountain

avenue a road with trees on both sides

average the typical or normal amount, in the middle

aviary a large cage where birds are kept

aviation the art of flying aircraft

avoid to keep away from a place or person (avoidance)

await to wait for

awake not asleep

awe great respect and fear (awesome)

awkward clumsy, not graceful, difficult

axe a tool with a sharp blade for cutting wood

axle the bar of wood or metal on which a wheel turns

B

baboon a large monkey

baby a human infant

bachelor an unmarried man

back 1. the rear portion of the body 2. to move towards the rear (backwards): *Luke backed the car into the garage.* 3. to place a bet on: *I was lucky to back the winning horse at the races.*

10 DICTIONARY

backbone the spinal column

background the part behind the main figures in a picture or scene

bacon the salted or smoked flesh of a pig

badger 1. to worry or annoy: *The children badgered their parents to take them to the zoo.*
2. a grey and white striped animal which lives in a burrow underground: *Badgers leave their burrows at night to look for food.*

baggage the bags and luggage people take when travelling

bail 1. to scoop water out of a boat
2. the little cross-piece bar laid on the tops of stumps in cricket
3. to set free on payment of a sum of money: *The judge set the bail at £1000.*

bake to cook in an oven; to harden by heat (baker)

bait pieces of food used to trap animals and fish

balance 1. a pair of scales for weighing: *Roger weighed the fruit on a balance.*
2. what is left over: *When you have bought your ticket, you can keep the balance of the money.*
3. to keep steady: *The acrobat kept his balance on the wire.*

balcony a platform with railings outside a window

bald with no hair on the head

ball 1. a round toy: *Bill kicked the ball over the fence.*
2. a dance attended by many people: *Cinderella went to the ball.*

ballet dancing and miming on stage to music

balloon a skin or container that can be filled with air so that it rises upwards

DICTIONARY 11

B

banana a long yellow fruit with a thick outer skin and cream coloured flesh

band 1. a connecting piece of metal, rubber or cloth: *Roy put a rubber band around the packet of letters.*
2. a group of the same kind of people: *The band of highwaymen met at the crossroads.*
3. a group of musicians: *The band played at the concert.*

bandage a long strip of material used to bind up wounds

bandit an armed robber

bang a short, loud sound

banish to send away for a long time (banishment)

banister the railing beside a staircase

bank 1. the ground at the edge of a river
2. a safe and secure building to keep money

banner a long flag

banquet a feast with lots of different foods

bar 1. to prevent or stop people (barrier): *The farmer barred the entrance to the field.*
2. a place where one can buy drinks: *Fred ordered a round of drinks at the bar.*
3. a block of wood or metal: *The explorers discovered gold bars and silver coins.*

barbecue to cook food over the glowing embers of a fire

barber a person who cuts men's hair

bare with no clothes on, uncovered

bargain something bought at a cheap price

barge a flat-bottomed boat for carrying bulk goods

bark 1. the sound made by a dog
2. the outer covering of a tree: *Pine trees have a thick, rough bark.*

barn a large farm building where corn and hay are stored

12 DICTIONARY

B

barrel a round wooden container

barter to exchange things instead of using money

base 1. the bottom part on which a thing rests (basic): *The base of the pillar was carved from stone.*
2. the place where one starts out from: *The army was based in Germany.*

basin a wide bowl for washing

basket a woven container

bat 1. a heavy wooden stick used to hit a ball: *The cricketer hit the ball hard with the bat.*
2. a small, mouse–like mammal which flies at night: *The bats made a squeaking noise in the cave.*

batch a collection of things

bath a large container to wash in (bathe)

batter 1. to beat against: *The waves battered against the cliffs during the storm.*
2. a mixture of flower, milk and eggs

battery a number of cells that store electricity

battle a fight between two armies

bawl to cry out loudly

bay 1. a curving part of the seashore: *The tide carried the ship into the bay.*

2. to howl like a hound or wolf: *The wolves bayed at the moon all night.*

bazaar an Eastern market place; a sale of goods for charity

beach the sand by the edge of the sea

beacon a warning light on a high place

beak the hard mouth of a bird

beam 1. a ray of light: *A beam of moonlight came through the curtains.*
2. a heavy wooden roof support

bean the flat, kidney–shaped seeds of various plants

DICTIONARY 13

B

bear/bore 1. to carry: *The man bore a grudge against his partner.* 2. to suffer: *I cannot bear to see animals in pain.* 3. a large animal with thick fur and small eyes: *Bears spend the winter asleep in their dens.*

beard the hair that grows on the chin and cheeks

beast an animal (beastly)

beauty pleasing to the eye or other senses (beautiful)

beaver an animal that gnaws trees to build a home in the middle of a lake

because for the reason that

beckon to invite a person to come near by a movement of the hand or finger

become/became to change into a different state or form

bee a small insect that lives in a hive and makes honey

beef the flesh of an ox, bull or cow

beer an alcoholic drink made from barley, hops, sugar and water

beetle insects with hard outer cases covering their bodies

before in front of; at an earlier time

beg to ask for charity (beggar, begging)

begin/began to start (beginning)

behave to act in a certain way (behaviour)

behind at the back of

belfry the part of a church tower where the bells hang

believe to have faith in (belief)

bell a hollow, cup–shaped metal vessel with a swinging hammer which makes a musical sound when it hits the sides

bellow to roar like a bull

14 DICTIONARY

B

belong to own (belongings)

below underneath

belt a narrow band worn around the waist

bench a long wooden seat

bend/bent 1. to force into a curve or angle: *Julie bent the wire into a circle.*
2. a curve e.g. in the road

berry the fruit of various bushes (berries)

berth the place on a quay where a ship ties up

beside at the side of

best the most skilful and excellent

better showing improvement, more useful

betray to be unfaithful or plot against (betrayal)

between in the middle of two; shared by two

beware to look out for and take care

bewilder to puzzle or confuse (bewilderment)

bicycle a machine with two wheels driven by pedals

bind to tie up or fasten together (bound)

biography the story of someone's life

bird a creature with feathers and wings to fly

birthday the day one is born

biscuit a thin sweet hard cake

bison a large American buffalo

bite/bit to cut, crush, seize or wound with the teeth

bitter a sharp, unpleasant taste

black the darkest colour, the opposite of white

blackmail money obtained from a person by threats to do them harm

blacksmith a person who makes horse shoes and iron tools

blade 1. a leaf or thin flat thing (a blade of grass)
2. a sharp cutting edge: *The smith sharpened the blade of the axe.*

blame to find fault with or accuse

blank empty, with nothing on it

blanket a warm covering

B

blast a rush of wind or air

blaze the light from something burning (blazing)

bleach to make something white by leaving it in the sun or soaking it in a chemical liquid

bleed/bled to lose blood

blend to mix two things well together

blind 1. unable to see: *The blind man had a guide dog.*
2. a window shade: *We pulled down the blinds to keep out the sun.*

blister a small area of raised skin filled with a watery fluid caused by a burn or something rubbing against the skin

blizzard a heavy snowstorm with a strong wind blowing

block 1. a solid mass (a block of wood)
2. to stop or prevent movement: *The road was blocked by all the traffic.*

blood the red liquid which the heart pumps around the body

bloodshot when the eye is red and sore

bloom to flower or produce blossom

blossom the flowers on a tree before the fruit

blouse a thin loose upper garment worn tucked in at the waist

blow/blew 1. to produce a current of air with the mouth or by the wind: *Hazel blew out the candles on her cake.*
2. a knock or a thump: *The woodcutter cut down the tree with one blow.*

blue one of the seven colours of the rainbow; the colour of a clear sky

bluff 1. to pretend, and make your intentions seem opposite to what they really are: *Don't believe him; he's only bluffing.*
2. a high bank or cliff, a headland

blunder a stupid mistake

blunt having an edge that is not sharp

blurred not clear, dim and indistinct

16 DICTIONARY

B

blush to become red in the face

boar a wild pig

board 1. a wooden plank (floor board)
2. the food supplied to a lodger (boarder, boarding school): *Jenny pays for both board and lodging.*
3. on a ship (on board)

boast to brag about something

boat a small open vessel that is moved by oars or sails

body the frame of a human or animal supported by the skeleton

body-guard a person who protects someone important

bog wet, soft, muddy ground (boggy)

boil 1. to cook by heating (boil an egg)
2. a small red swelling on the skin

bolt 1. to run away quickly: *When the horse bolted, the rider fell off.*
2. a metal bar to fasten a door

bomb to explode a container filled with explosives (bomber)

bone the hard tissue which forms the skeleton of humans and animals (bony)

bonfire a large fire in the open air

book 1. to make a reservation in advance (booking): *Will booked a seat on the plane to Paris.*
2. printed sheets of paper bound together (storybook)

boom 1. a long pole to stretch the bottom of a sail
2. a deep, hollow sound

boomerang a curved wooden weapon that returns to the thrower

boot a covering for the foot and ankle

border the edge of anything

DICTIONARY 17

B

bore 1. a dull, uninteresting person or subject (boring): *The students found the lecture boring.* 2. to drill a hole into something: *The woodpecker bored a hole in the tree trunk.*

borrow to get something on loan

bottle a container for liquids

bottom the lowest part of anything

bough a branch of a tree

boulder a large rock or stone

bound a leap or jump

boundary the line that divides one place from another

bow (say bow) to bend the head in respectful greeting

bow (say boh) 1. a curved weapon used to shoot arrows 2. a stick tied with many horsehairs used to play the violin or cello

3. a way of tying a ribbon to look pretty

bowl 1. a deep, round basin 2. to throw a ball in a game of cricket (bowler)

box 1. to fight with padded gloves in a ring (boxer; boxing ring) 2. a container with square corners

boy a male child

bracelet an ornament worn around the wrist

bracken a kind of wild fern often found on hillsides

brain the mass of nervous tissue inside the skull used for thinking

brake to slow a moving object down

bramble a wild, thorny blackberry bush

branch 1. a limb or a tree or shrub 2. one of a chain of shops or businesses: *There was a branch of Smiths in the town.* 3. a smaller part or a river or railway: *We had to change from the main railway line to a branch line.*

18 DICTIONARY

B

brave 1. fearless, courageous (bravery) 2. a Red Indian warrior

brawl a noisy fight or quarrel

bray the sound made by a donkey

bread food made by mixing flour and water and baking the dough

break/broke to shatter into small pieces (breakage)

breaker a large wave

breakfast the first meal of the day

breathe to take air in and out of our lungs (breath, breathing)

breeze a light and gentle wind (breezy)

bribe a payment or gift to make a person do something that is wrong (bribery)

brick clay shaped into a block that is hardened by fire and later used in building a house

bride a woman on the day she gets married (bridal)

bridge a building with arches to cross over rivers and valleys

brief short

bright 1. shining, giving out light: *The sun shone brightly.* 2. clever, happy, cheerful: *Sarah is a bright girl who always does well in school.*

brilliant very bright, sparkling or very clever

brim the rim or border of anything; the edge of a hat

bring/brought to carry, to fetch

brink the top edge of a steep slope

brisk quick and lively

bristle the stiff hair on a brush

brittle easily broken

broad wide; the opposite of narrow (breadth)

broadcast to send out talks, music and plays on the radio or on television

bronze a metal made of copper and tin

brooch a decoration with a pin to fasten it to the wearer's clothes

brook a small stream

broom a brush with a long handle for sweeping floors

DICTIONARY 19

B

brother a male born of the same parents

brown a dark colour made by mixing red, yellow and black; the colour of mud

bruise a blue–black mark on the skin made by a knock or injury which does not break the skin

brush a tool made of bristles, twigs or feather used to sweep dirt or untangle knots in the hair

bubble a very light, shiny ball made by blowing air into soap and water (bubbly)

bucket a large metal or plastic container for carrying water

build/built to make a house, office or church from stone or bricks (builder, building)

bulb 1. the roots of some spring flowers (daffodil bulb)

2. a thin glass globe with a wire inside that glows when electricity is passed through (electric light bulb)

bulge to swell out

bulk size (bulky)

bull a male cow, ox, elephant, and other animals

bulldozer a machine for moving and levelling earth

bullet a small piece of metal fired from a gun

bully a person who is rough and unkind to a weaker person

bump to knock against something (bumper)

bunch to group or tie similar things together

bundle a number of things bound together

bungalow a house with all the rooms on the ground floor

bunk a broad shelf used as a seat by day and a bed at night

buoy a floating marker fixed in position on the sea bed to mark the channel for ships (buoyant)

20 DICTIONARY

burden something that is heavy to carry (burdensome)

burglar a thief who breaks into a house (burglary)

burn/burnt to destroy by fire

burrow to dig a hole in the earth

burst to fly apart and break into pieces

bury to put in the ground (burial)

bush a plant like a small tree, with many small branches (bushy)

business work that earns a person money

busy full of work or activity

butcher a person who cut up dead animals and sells them for food

butter an edible yellow fat made from the cream of milk

butterfly an insect with brightly coloured wings

button a knob sewn on clothes to fasten them together

buy/bought to pay money to get something

bypass a road which goes around the outside of a town

byre a stable where cows are kept

cabbage a green leafy garden vegetable

cabin 1. a small wooden hut
2. a room on board ship

cable a strong metal rope

café a place where one can buy tea or coffee to drink

cage a box or container made of metal bars for keeping animals or birds

cake a kind of sweet bread

calculate to count; to work out the figures (calculator)

calendar a way of showing the day, weeks, and months of a year

calf the young of a cow (calves)

call to shout or cry out

calm to soothe and quieten

camel an animal that can live for many days without drinking

DICTIONARY 21

C

camera a box with film inside used to take photographs

camouflage to make something difficult to see

camp a collection of tents (camper)

canal an artificial river

canary a small, yellow song bird

cancel to stop something happening; to cross out (cancellation)

candle a stick of wax with thread inside that burns and gives out light

cannibal a person who eats human flesh

cannon a very large gun

canoe a very light boat that is moved by paddles

canter to gallop gently

canvas a coarse cloth used to make tents and sails

capital 1. the chief city of a country: *Paris is the capital of France.*
2. a large letter: *A sentence should begin with a capital letter.*

capsize to turn a boat upside down

captain the chief officer on a boat or aeroplane; the leader of a group.

capture to catch or take by force (captive)

car a wheeled machine that is driven along roads

caravan 1. a house on wheels: *Jenny stayed in a caravan on holiday.*
2. a large group of traders that travel across the desert

carcass the dead body of an animal

card 1. stiff paper (post-card)
2. a printed greeting (Christmas card)
3. a small shaped piece of paper printed with symbols on one side (playing card)

cardboard a thick stiff paper used to make boxes

cardigan a light woollen jacket

C

care 1. to look after; take trouble over: *Dave took care of the puppy when his mother went out.*
2. to like: *Tom does not care for coffee; he prefers tea.*
3. to feel anxious about: *I don't care if you are not feeling well.*

career 1. a person's work throughout their life: *Julie took up dentistry as a career.*
2. to rush wildly about: *When the driver lost control, the car careered all over the road.*

cargo the goods carried by ship

carnival an open air festival with games, sports and music

carol a Christmas song or hymn

carpenter a person who makes things from wood

carpet a woven covering for floors

carrot a garden vegetable with a long orange root

carry to take from one place to another (carrier, carriage)

cart 1. a two-wheeled vehicle with long poles which is pulled by hand

2. to take away something heavy

carton a box made of card

cartoon drawings that are usually funny

carve 1. to cut a design into wood or stone (carving): *Jim carved his name on the tree.*
2. to cut into thin slices: *Jane carved the joint of beef.*

case 1. an example or happening: *Joan took an anorak in case she got cold.*
2. a container (clock case)

cash paper money and coins (cashier)

casserole a stew cooked in the oven

DICTIONARY 23

C

cassette a container for magnetic tape on which music and speech is recorded

castaway a shipwrecked person

castle a fort or strong house that can be defended against an enemy

casual careless, happening by chance

catalogue a list of things arranged in order

catapult a toy with a rubber loop which can be used to shoot stones

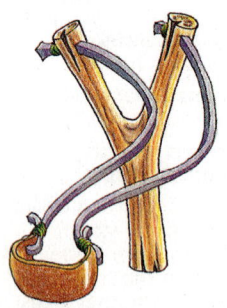

catch/caught 1. to run after and seize: *The policeman caught the thief.*
2. a bolt or lock: *The catch on the case was broken and the lid fell open.*
3. a problem or snag: *The catch is that we must walk back home after the fair.*

caterpillar the stage of life for a moth or butterfly before it grows its wings

cathedral a very large church

cattle cows, bulls and oxen

cauldron a very large metal pot for cooking over a fire

cauliflower a garden vegetable with white flowers grouped tightly together in a single large head

cause to produce a result or effect

caution to warn; to take care (cautious)

cavalry soldiers that ride horses

cave a hollow place underground

cease to stop

ceiling the inside roof of a room

celebrate to mark by a festival or event (celebration)

C

cell 1. a small room in a prison or monastery 2. the smallest unit of living matter: *Our bodies are made of millions of cells.*

cellar an underground storeroom

cello a large stringed instrument which plays deep notes

cement 1. a mixture used by builders to hold bricks together 2. to join closely

cemetery a graveyard where the dead are buried

centre the middle point of something, especially of a circle (central)

century a period of one hundred years

cereal any kind of grain, such as corn or wheat, that is used for food

ceremony a way of doing something very formally in public

certain sure, without any doubt

certificate a written statement of a fact

chain a series of metal rings linked together

chair a seat with a back

chalk a soft white stone which crumbles into a powder easily

challenge to invite to a contest

champion 1. a person who fights for another: *The queen chose the black knight as her champion.* 2. a person who wins all the prizes in games or sports: *Luke was the champion swimmer in the school.*

chance the possibility or opportunity

change 1. to alter or become different: *Sarah changed her shoes when she got home.* 2. to take or use one thing instead of another: *Jean changed her dirty dress for a clean one.* 3. small coins rather than big notes of money

channel the deep part of a river or harbour

chaos great disorder or confusion (chaotic)

chapel a small building used for worship

chapter one of the parts which divides up a book or story

C

character the kind of person one is

charge 1. to ask for money in payment: *The garage charged a lot of money to repair the car.* 2. to ride against the enemy on horseback: *The horsemen charged down the field of battle.*

charity to give help to the poor and needy (charitable)

charm 1. to please people by pleasant behaviour (charming): *Ruth's manners charmed her great aunt.* 2. a magic spell or potion to ward off evil: *Ken wore a silver charm on a chain around his neck.*

chart a map for ships to find their way at sea

chase to run after and try to catch

chat to talk in a friendly way (chatter)

chauffeur a person who is paid to drive a private car

cheap costing very little

cheat to deceive or do something that is dishonest

check to make sure something is correct

cheek 1. the fleshy side of the face below the eyes: *Ian had red cheeks.* 2. to speak in a saucy, impudent way (cheeky): *Margaret was very cheeky when talking to her teacher.*

cheer 1. to give a shout of praise or joy 2. to make happier: *Bess tried to cheer her friend up.*

cheese the curds separated from milk and pressed into a solid mass

chemist 1. a person who sells medicines 2. a scientist who works with different substances and elements (chemistry)

cheque a written order to a bank asking them to pay a sum of money

C

cherry a tree with small sweet fruits that have a large stone in the centre

chess a game played by two people on a board with 32 pieces or chessmen

chest 1. a large box with a lid
2. the upper front part of the human body

chew to bite into small pieces with one's teeth

chicken a hen

chief a leader or head person

child a young human person (children)

chill to make something cool

chime a musical sound of a bell ringing

chimney the passage through which the smoke of a fire escapes upwards

chimpanzee a large African ape

chin the part of the face below the mouth

chip a small piece cut or broken off

chocolate a dark brown powder made from the seeds of the cacao plant and used to make a smooth sweet or drink

choir a group of singers (choral)

choke to have difficulty in swallowing

choose/chose 1. to pick out from among others (choice): *Ben chose a yellow sweater.*
2. to decide: *Ann chose to go to Italy on holiday.*

chop 1. to cut into pieces
2. a piece of meat (lamb chop)

chorus the part of a song that everyone sings together at the end of each verse

christen to name a child in a religious ceremony

church a building for worshipping God

cider a drink made from crushed apples

cinder a piece of coal that is still glowing

cinema a hall or theatre where one can watch films

DICTIONARY 27

C

circle a completely round shape or ring (circular)

circumference the line around the edge of a circle

circus a show in a tent of performing animals, acrobats and clowns

citizen a person who lives in a city

city a large town

civilian anyone who is not in the Army, Navy or Air Force

civilisation in a state of possessing knowledge, culture and education

claim to ask for something that one has a right to

clap to bring the hands together as a sign of approval

class a group of people or things of the same sort

clatter to make a rattling sound

claw the sharp nail of a bird or animal

clay a soft kind of earth which goes hard when baked in an oven

clean to remove dust and dirt

clear 1. bright and easily seen through
2. free of any blocks: *The road was clear of traffic.*

clerk an office worker

clever able and intelligent

client a customer

cliff a high wall of rock near the edge of the sea

climate the sort of weather a place usually has

climb to go or clamber up

cloak a long loose outer garment that protects or hides the clothes underneath

clock an instrument to measure time

clog 1. to block up: *The pipe was clogged up with earth.*
2. a wooden shoe

28 DICTIONARY

close (say kloze) to shut or end (closure)

close (say klose) very near to

cloth woven material made of wool, cotton, etc

clothes what people wear (clothing)

cloud a mass of water vapour one can see floating in the sky

clown a person who says and does funny things to make people laugh

club 1. a heavy wooden stick used as a weapon: *The giant raised his club, but Jack escaped.* 2. a group of people who meet together to do things that they are all interested in: *Darrel and James both belong to a sports club.*

clue a piece of information that helps solve a mystery

clump a number of plants growing close together

clumsy slow and awkward in movement

cluster a bunch or collection of things

clutch 1. to hold tightly: *The mother clutched her baby to save it from falling.* 2. the pedal inside a car which disconnects the engine

coach 1. to teach or help another to become good at a game (coaching) 2. a long-distance bus

coal a black substance made of fossilized plants that we dig out of the earth to burn

coarse rough to the taste or feel

coast the land at the edge of the sea

coat 1. an outer garment worn on top of one's other clothing 2. to cover over (coating): *Bill coated the engine with oil.*

coax to persuade

cobweb the threads spun by a spider to catch insects

DICTIONARY 29

C

cock 1. a male hen
2. to raise and get ready (cock a gun)
3. to set at an angle (cocked hat)
4. a tap to stop the flow of liquids (stop cock)

coconut the fruit of the coconut palm tree

code a set of letters or symbols used to send messages

coffee a drink made from the dried and ground seeds of a coffee tree

coffin a wooden box in which a dead person is buried

coil to wind round in a ring

coin a round piece of metal stamped and used as money

coincidence an unexpected event that happens by chance

cold not warm, with no heat

collapse to suddenly fall down

collar something worn around the neck

collect to gather together (collector, collection)

colliery where coal is mined

colony a group of people or animals that live together

colour the tint or shade, something that is not white

colt a young horse

column a pillar or support

comb to smooth the hair and get out the tangles

combine harvester a machine for cutting or harvesting ripe crops

come/came to move towards

comedian a person that makes others laugh (comedy)

comet a heavenly body with a tail of light

30 DICTIONARY

comfort to help somebody who is unhappy (comforting, comfortable)

comic 1. funny 2. a newspaper with only cartoon drawings

command to order (commandment)

comment to make a remark

committee a group of people elected for a special purpose

common 1. a piece of ground open to everybody 2. usual, ordinary, well-known: *A daisy is a common flower in gardens and parks.*

communicate to pass on a message (communication)

company a group of people

compare to look at two things and see if they are the same or different (comparison)

compartment a part that is divided off (railway compartment)

compass an instrument with a needle that always points north and so helps people find their way

compete to try to do better than others and win the prize (competition)

complain to find fault with and say that something is wrong (complaint)

complete to finish, with all the parts there (completion)

complicate to make more difficult (complication)

compose to make up; to arrange or put in order (composer, composition)

computer a machine which sorts information when given a set of commands

conceal to hide (concealment)

conceit having a high opinion of yourself

concentrate to think hard about something (concentration)

DICTIONARY 31

C

concern 1. to be of interest or involved in: *John's hobby was learning about all the things that concern animals.*
2. worry, or a feeling of anxiety: *Sheila's mother was very concerned when she did not arrive home.*

concert a musical entertainment

condemn to say that a person is guilty (condemnation)

condition 1. a state of repair: *My bicycle is in a poor condition.*
2. part of an agreement that must be carried out: *Sean's dad allowed him to go to the match on condition that he came straight home afterwards.*

conduct (say con<u>dukt</u>) to lead or show the way (conductor): *Jean conducted the orchestra.*

conduct (say <u>con</u>dukt) behaviour: *Bill got a merit award for good conduct.*

cone 1. the fruit of a fir tree
2. a shape that thins down to a point from a circular base (conical): *The road was blocked off by traffic cones.*

confess to admit to having done something wrong (confession)

confide to tell a secret (confidant)

confidence a feeling of faith or trust (confident)

confiscate to take away by power or right (confiscation)

conflict (say kon<u>flikt</u>) to fight or struggle against: *Bill's ideas conflicted with his brother's.*

conflict (say <u>kon</u>flikt) a fight: *The conflict lasted all day.*

confuse to mix or muddle up (confusion)

congratulate to wish someone joy or pleasure (congratulations)

conifer a tree that bears its seeds in cones

conjure to do magic tricks (conjuror)

32 DICTIONARY

connect to join together (connection)

conquer to defeat in battle (conqueror, conquest)

conscience a feeling that knows right from wrong (conscientious)

conscious knowing what is going on (consciousness)

consent to agree

consequence following on as a result

consider 1. to think about (consideration): *John considered whether to apply for the job.*
2. to hold an opinion: *Bob considered that his uncle was a fool.*

console to comfort or make happier (consolation)

constant 1. unchanging, without stopping: *It rained constantly all week.*
2. faithful: *Fay's dog was her constant companion.*

construct to build or join up the parts (construction)

contain to hold; to have as part of itself (container)

content (say <u>kon</u>tent) the parts or amount inside: *Fred spilled the contents of the glass.*

content (say kon<u>tent</u>) to be happy, pleased: *Sarah was content with the result of her exam.*

contest to fight or struggle against (contestant)

continent a large mass of land (continental)

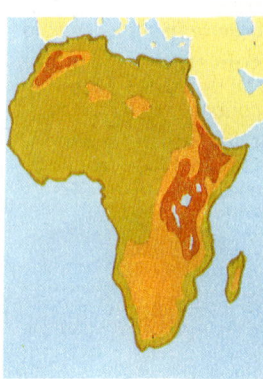

continue to carry on without a break (continuation)

contradict to say the opposite (contradiction)

contrast (say <u>kon</u>trast) a great difference between things: *Jane's writing was very neat in contrast to her brother's.*

contrast (say kon<u>trast</u>) to compare things and bring out the difference: *Joe contrasted his dog with Amanda's.*

DICTIONARY 33

C

control to check or keep in order

convenience something useful (convenient)

convent a building where nuns live

converse (say kon<u>verse</u>) to talk with (conversation): *The friends conversed quietly in the corner.*

converse (say <u>kon</u>verse) the opposite: *The converse of tall is short.*

cook a person who prepares food (cooking, cookery)

cool not too hot

copy to make a thing like something else, to imitate

cork a stopper for a bottle made from the bark of a cork tree

corkscrew an instrument with a screw used to take corks out of bottles

corn 1. a cereal crop of oats, wheat, or barley 2. a hardened area of the skin

corner a bend, or the point where two walls meet

cornflakes a breakfast cereal

corpse a dead body

correct to mark as right, free from faults (correction)

corridor a passage in a building

cost to have as a price

cosy warm and comfortable

cottage a small simple house in the country

cotton thread made from the soft fibres inside the cotton seed

cough to make a noisy rough sound when trying to clear one's throat (coughing)

count to number or include

34 DICTIONARY

country any land outside towns; the land of a nation

couple 1. a pair 2. to join together (coupling): *Henry coupled up the horsebox to the back of the car.*

courage brave and fearless (courageous)

course 1. a movement in space and in time: *The ship's course was due north.* 2. a track for racing (race course) 3. a series of lessons or lectures: *Susan took a course in car maintenance.*

court 1. an uncovered area surrounded by buildings 2. a space laid out for sport (tennis court) 3. to seek the favour of (courtier)

cousin the son or daughter of an uncle or aunt

cover to protect or put a layer over

cow 1. the female of many animals such as ox, elephant, whale, etc. 2. to frighten (coward, cowardice)

crab an animal with pincers and a hard case to protect its body

crack 1. to make a sharp noise: *The ringmaster cracked the whip.* 2. to almost break: *The glass was cracked.*

crane 1. a machine for lifting up heavy objects

2. a kind of bird with a long neck 3. to stretch one's neck so as to be able to see: *Ted craned over the heads of the crowd to watch the match.*

crash to hit something very hard and make a loud noise

crawl to move on hands and knees

crayon to colour something using a wax or chalk stick

DICTIONARY 35

C

crazy mad, silly

cream the fatty substance within milk

create to make something that did not exist before (creation)

creature something living, not a plant or man

creep/crept to move along with the body close to the ground

crescent the shape of a new moon

crest 1. the bunch of feathers on a bird's head

2. the top of a wave

crew the people who manage a ship or aeroplane

cricket 1. a game played with a bat and ball 2. a small chirping insect that lives in grass

crime an act that is against the law (criminal)

crimson a deep red colour

cripple to make lame or make difficult to walk

crisp something that is brittle and breaks with a snap

criticise to say what you think about something (critic, criticism)

crochet to make something with a hook and thread

crocodile a large lizard–like animal with sharp teeth

crocus a small brightly coloured flower that grows from a bulb

crooked bent or twisted

crop 1. the plants grown in a field or garden: *The crop of wheat was ready to harvest.*
2. to cut very short: *The hairdresser cropped off all Mary's hair.*

cross 1. to go from one side the other (crossing)
2. angry, or annoyed
3. a shape made by one line going across another: *The teacher put a cross against the wrong answer.*

36 DICTIONARY

crossword a word puzzle of filling in the white squares from the clues

crow 1. to make a sound like a cock 2. a large bird with black feathers

crowd to crush together into a space

crown to place a golden circle around the head of a king or queen

cruel very unkind, causing pain (cruelty)

cruise to take a holiday on a ship that travels from port to port

crush to squeeze and break

cry/cried to call out, to weep

cub the young of some animals

cucumber a long green fleshy fruit used in salads

cuddle to hold close or hug

culprit a person who has done something wrong

cultivate to grow crops (cultivation)

cunning clever in a sly, deceitful way

cupboard a piece of furniture with shelves or rails

curb 1. the edge of a pavement 2. to control or check: *Sam tried to curb his temper.*

cure to make well again

curious 1. strange, odd: *Barbara wore a curious straw hat shaped like a bird.* 2. eager to know (curiosity): *The children were curious to know what was inside the box.*

curl 1. to twist or bend into a curved shape: *The dried leaves curled up.* 2. a section of hair in a ring shape

currant 1. the soft fruit of various bushes (blackcurrant) 2. small dried grape

current 1. the flow of water in a river or sea 2. going on at the moment: *The current series on television is about dinosaurs.*

curse to wish someone evil, to swear at

curtain a long piece of cloth hung from the top of a window

curve to bend without angles

cushion a bag or case filled with soft stuffing

DICTIONARY 37

D

dagger a short, two-edged sword

dairy the place where milk and butter are kept cool, or are sold

daisy a common wild flower growing chiefly in grass

damage to harm or spoil

damp slightly wet

dance to move to music

danger in a position to cause harm, injury, or damage (dangerous)

dare to be brave enough to do something

dark with no light

dart 1. to move very quickly: *The fish darted through the reeds.* 2. a small pointed weapon thrown by hand

date 1. the day or time when a thing happened 2. the small sweet fruit of a date palm

daughter a female child

dawdle to do something slowly and without interest

dawn when the sun rises

day the period from sunrise to sunset (daily)

daze to confuse and upset

dazzle to make almost blind for a short time

dead without life

deaf unable to hear

dear 1. much loved 2. expensive

death when something stops living

debate to argue or discuss a subject (debater)

debt something one owes to another person

decay to rot away

deceive to make a person believe what is not true (deceit, deception)

December the last month of the year

decent suitable, respectable, good enough

decide to make up one's mind (decision)

38 DICTIONARY

declare to make known publicly (declaration)

decorate to make more beautiful (decoration)

decrease to become less

deed something one does, an act

deep far down below the surface (depth)

deer a grass-eating animal, the male of which has antlers

defeat to overcome or win a fight or struggle

defend to protect or fight off (defendant, defence)

definite clear and without doubt

defy to challenge or disobey on purpose (defiance)

degree a measure of temperature

delay 1. to keep back and make late: *The train was delayed by half an hour.*
2. to put off until later: *Bill delayed his departure until Jane arrived.*

delicate finely made, dainty

delicious very nice to eat, tasting very good

delight to give great pleasure to

deliver 1. to hand over (delivery): *The postman delivers the letters every morning.*
2. to set free from danger (deliverance): *The prisoners were delivered from danger.*

demand to ask for firmly

demolish to pull down or destroy (demolition)

dense thick, tightly packed together

dentist a person who looks after teeth (dental)

deny to say that a statement is untrue (denial)

depart to go away or leave (departure)

depend to trust or rely on (dependence)

depress to press down, to lower (depression)

descend to go down, to sink (descendant)

DICTIONARY 39

D

describe to give a picture of something (description)

desert (say de<u>sert</u>) a place where very little grows because of lack of water or extreme cold: *Very little rain falls in a desert.*

desert (say de<u>sert</u>) to leave or abandon (desertion): *There was nobody near the deserted house.*

deserve to earn something by doing something well

design to draw a plan or sketch of how a thing should be made

desk a table for reading or writing

despair to have no more hope

desperate very serious or beyond hope

dessert a sweet course at the end of a meal

destination the place to which one travels or sends things

destroy to ruin or pull down (destruction)

detail a very small part

detect to find out (detective, detection)

determine to settle or decide (determination)

detest to hate and dislike

develop to grow or unfold gradually (development)

devil an evil spirit

devour to eat greedily and completely

diagram a drawing or plan made to show something in outline

dial 1. the face of a clock or instrument 2. to press the numbers on a telephone in order to make a call: *Peter dialled his home phone number to speak to his parents.*

diamond a colourless precious stone that sparkles brilliantly

diary a record of what has happened every day

dictate to tell someone what to say or write (dictation)

dictionary a book containing an alphabetical list of words and their meanings

die to stop living

40 DICTIONARY

D

diesel a kind of engine which runs on a heavy oil

diet to eat less so as to lose weight

differ to disagree or be unlike in appearance (difference)

difficult hard to do or understand, not easy (difficulty)

digest to change food in the stomach into small particles which can be absorbed in the bloodstream (digestion)

dignity solemn, calm behaviour

dilapidated in a bad state or poor repair

dilute to make thinner or weaker (dilution)

dimension measurement

diminish to become less, weaker or smaller

dine to eat a formal meal (dinner)

dinghy a small boat with oars or sails

dingy dull and shabby

dinosaur a large prehistoric animal

direct 1. in a straight line: *We took the most direct road to London.* 2. to tell someone the way to go (direction): *Can you direct me to the station?* 3. to tell people what to do (director): *The director told him to type out the letter.*

dirt dust and mud; a filthy substance (dirty)

disagree to quarrel or have a different opinion (disagreement)

disappear to vanish from sight (disappearance)

disappoint to be sad that something has not happened (disappointment)

disapprove to think something is not right (disapproval)

D

disaster a sudden and terrible happening

disc a flat circular plate

discipline training how to behave

disconnect to separate or unfasten (disconnection)

discourage to make less hopeful, to dishearten (discouragement)

discover to find out something new (discovery)

discuss to talk about (discussion)

disease an illness

disgrace to be out of favour or thought badly of

disguise to change shape or appearance

disgust a feeling of dislike and loathing

dish a shallow plate made of china, etc.

dishonest not honest or trustworthy

disinfect to kill off any germs carrying disease (disinfectant)

dislike to not like or get on with

disloyal not loyal or trustworthy

dismal gloomy or miserable

dismiss to send away (dismissal)

disobey not to do what one is told, or to do the opposite (disobedience)

dispatch to send off

display to put on show

displease to annoy or make angry (displeasure)

dispute to argue or quarrel

dissatisfied not pleased or satisfied

dissolve to melt in a liquid

dissuade to advise not to, persuade against (dissuasion)

distance the space between two points

distinct clear, easily seen or heard

distinguish to tell the difference between two things

distress to worry or suffer

distribute to divide among several (distribution)

district an area of land

distrust not to trust or have faith in

42 DICTIONARY

disturb to trouble or interrupt (disturbance)

ditch a long narrow space dug in the ground beside a road to carry away water

dive to plunge into water head first (diver, diving)

divide to split up into bits (division)

dizzy feeling giddy, that everything is spinning around

dock 1. a place where ships are loaded and unloaded
2. an enclosed space in a law court where the prisoner stands
3. a weed

doctor a person who looks after sick people

dodge to get out of the way of something

doll a child's toy

dolphin a large mammal that is like a small whale

dome the curved roof on a building

domestic to do with the house or home

donation a gift, usually of money

donkey an animal smaller than a horse that carries loads

doom fate

door an opening that can be closed off

dormant sleeping, not active

dormouse a small animal which sleeps all winter

dose the amount of medicine to be taken at one time

double 1. twice as much: *The book cost double the amount of the magazine.*
2. a person who is exactly like another person: *Mary looked so like Jane she could have been her double.*
3. two parts or layers (double doors)

DICTIONARY 43

D

doubt to be uncertain or not willing to believe

dough a mixture of flour and water that can be baked to make bread

down 1. in a lower position: *Tom ran down the steps.*
2. the soft feathers of birds

doze to sleep lightly, to be half asleep

dozen twelve of anything

drab dull and dreary

drag to pull along behind

dragon a magic reptile that can breathe smoke and fire

dragonfly an insect with brilliantly coloured wings, large eyes and a long slender body

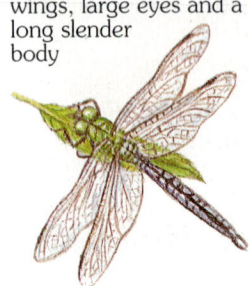

drain to let liquid run away

drake a male duck

drama a play for acting in the theatre

draught a current of air

draw/drew 1. to pull towards one: *The horse draws the cart.*
2. to make a picture: *Henry drew a picture of an elephant*
3. the end of a game when both sides are equal: *football match ended in a draw.*

drawer a box which slides in and out of a piece of furniture

dread to fear or be afraid of

dream to have thoughts and visions while asleep

dress 1. to put on clothes
2. a garment worn by girls and women

drift 1. to be carried along by the wind or tide: *The boat drifted out to sea.*
2. a pile of anything heaped up by the wind: *The car got stuck in the snow drift.*

drill to pierce or bore a hole through

drink/drank to swallow a liquid

drive/drove 1. to guide and control a vehicle (driver): *Jim learned to drive when he was very young.*
2. the path up to a front door: *The drive from the front gate was edged with flowers.*

D

drizzle to rain gently

dromedary a kind of camel with one hump

drone 1. a male honey bee
2. a deep humming sound

droop to hang down or grow weak

drop 1. to let something fall: *Jenny dropped the glass and it broke.*
2. a small amount of liquid: *Add a few drops of food colouring to the clay.*

drought a long period without rain

drown to die by being kept under water and not being able to breathe (drowning)

drowsy sleepy

drug a medicine

drum a musical instrument with a thin stretched skin which is beaten by a stick or the hand

dry not wet, with no moisture

duck 1. a domesticated water fowl
2. to dodge or avoid

duel a fight between two persons

dull not bright, not sharp

dumb unable to speak

dune a bank or hill of sand

dungeon an underground prison in a castle

dusk when the sun has set and it is nearly dark

dust to clean off small specks of matter (duster)

dustbin a container for rubbish

duty what one ought to do

duvet a bed covering stuffed with feathers

dwarf a very small animal, plant or person

dwell to live somewhere (dwelling)

dye to change the colour

DICTIONARY 45

E

eager keen, enthusiastic

eagle a large bird of prey

ear 1. the organ you use to hear with 2. the head of corn which carries the grain

early in good time, before the time expected

earn to get paid for work done (earnings)

earth 1. the soil or ground
2. the planet on which we live

earthquake a shaking of the earth's surface caused by underground movements of the earth's crust

easel a wooden frame an artist uses to support pictures whilst painting

east the part of the horizon where the sun rises (eastern)

easy not difficult

eat to swallow food

eaves the bottom part of a sloping roof that hangs over the walls

eavesdropper a person who listens to a private conversation

ebb to flow back

ebony a very hard black wood

eccentric odd or queer

echo when sound is reflected or bounced back to the listener

eclipse when the moon comes between the earth and the sun

edge 1. the border or outside of anything: *Jenny paddled in the waves at the edge of the sea.*
2. the cutting part of a blade: *Mark sharpened the edge of the blade.*

edible anything that can be eaten

educate to teach or train (education)

eel a fish with a long, thin body like a snake

eerie weird or frightening

effect a result (effective)

efficient able to produce a result or do things well

E

effort to try hard, to struggle to do something

egg 1. an oval body laid by birds inside which the young bird develops 2. to urge or encourage: *Ben egged on his friend to win the prize.*

eject to throw out (ejection)

elaborate complicate, with many details or ornaments

elastic a material which stretches and can spring back to its original shape

elbow the joint in the arm which bends

elder 1. an older person

2. a kind of tree with white flowers and purple berries

elect to choose (election)

electricity power which can produce heat, light and movement (electrician)

elegant fashionable, graceful

elephant a large animal with a long nose or trunk, and ivory tusks

elf a little fairy with pointed ears

embankment a mound of earth built up at the side of a river to carry a railway

embarrass to make uncomfortable or shy

embers pieces of coal in a fire which have not quite burned out

embrace to hug or kiss

embroider to decorate by sewing with different stitches

emerald a precious stone of a green colour

emerge to come out of or come into sight (emergence)

emergency an unexpected happening that makes it necessary to act quickly to avoid danger

emigrate to leave one's own country and go and live in another country (emigration)

DICTIONARY 47

E

emit to give off or send out (emission)

emotion a strong feeling such as sorrow, happiness, etc.

emphasise to draw attention to (emphasis)

employ to pay a person money in return for doing work (employee, employment)

empty with nothing inside

emu a flightless bird that lives in Australia

enamel a hard, shiny covering

enchant to please or delight (enchantment)

encircle to make a circle around

enclose 1. to shut in (enclosure): *The giant enclosed his garden with a high fence.* 2. to put in: *Jill enclosed a photograph with her letter.*

encore a cry from an audience asking for a repeat of a song or piece

encounter to meet

encourage to give someone courage or hope

encyclopedia a book containing information about many different subjects

endanger to place in danger

endeavour to try hard

endure to bear or put up with (endurance)

enemy a person who is hostile to another

energy the power to do work, to be very active

engine a machine (engineer, engineering)

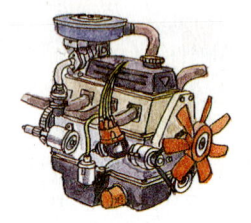

enjoy to like or find pleasure in (enjoyment)

enlarge to make bigger or larger (enlargement)

enormous very large indeed

enough as much as one needs, the right amount

48 DICTIONARY

E

enrage to make very angry

enrol to become a member of a group or society (enrolment)

enter to go in (entrance)

entertain to amuse and give pleasure to (entertainment)

enthusiasm having a great interest in (enthusiastic)

entire complete, whole

entreat to beg or ask eagerly (entreaty)

envelop to cover or surround, to wrap up

envelope a paper covering used to send a letter through the post

envy to be jealous of

epidemic an illness that affects many people at the same time

equal the same in size or numbers (equality)

equator the circle that divides the earth into it's northern and southern hemispheres (equatorial)

equip to fit out or supply with everything that is necessary (equipment)

equivalent equal in value though not exactly alike

era a long period of time

erase to rub out

errand a short journey to deliver a message or do something for another person

erupt to throw out or break through (eruption)

escalator a moving staircase

escape to get free, to get away

escort to go with or accompany

essential absolutely necessary

establish to set up or get going (establishment)

estimate to form an opinion of the value, size or weight (estimation)

estuary a wide river mouth

evacuate to go away from, leave (evacuation)

evade to escape from (evasion)

evaporate to dry up (evaporation)

DICTIONARY 49

E

even 1. flat, level, smooth: *The lawn was even and had no bumps in it.* 2. a number that can be divided by two

evening the time of day when the sun has set

event a happening

eventually in the end, at last

every each of all, not leaving anyone or thing out

evident clear and easily seen (evidence)

evil wicked, wrong, sinful

ewe a female sheep

exact correct, accurate

exaggerate to give something greater importance than it deserves (exaggeration)

examine to look at closely (examination)

example something that illustrates a general rule, a model

exasperate to make cross or annoy (exasperation)

excavate to dig out (excavation)

excellent very good

except to leave out (exception)

exchange to swop or change one thing for another

excite to stir up or cause strong feelings (excitement)

exclaim to say aloud in surprise (exclamation)

excuse (say eks<u>cuze</u>) to forgive

excuse (say ekscuse) to offer an apology for a fault

execute 1. to put to death by law (execution): *King Charles was executed.* 2. to carry out an action or task: *Fred executed the job he was given very well.*

exercise to move the limbs and body to make one more healthy

exhaust 1. to tire out (exhaustion): *After their trip to the beach, Sally was exhausted.* 2. waste gases from a car

exhibit to show or put on display (exhibition)

exile to send away to another country

exist to be, to live (existence)

exit the way out

expand to get larger and take up more space (expansion)

50 DICTIONARY

E

expect to look for and believe that something will happen (expectation)

expedition a group of people who set out for a definite purpose, such as an exploration

expensive costing a lot of money

experience knowledge gained from all that a person has seen, heard or done

experiment to test things out

expert having a great deal of knowledge

explain to make clear, give the meaning of (explanation)

explode to burst with a loud noise (explosion)

explore to travel and discover new lands (exploration)

export to send goods to other countries

express 1. to show or tell one's feelings (expression) 2. very fast

exquisite very delicate and beautiful

extend to stretch out in area or length (extent, extension)

exterior the outside

external on the outside

extinct died out

extinguish to put out flames (extinguisher)

extra in addition to

extract to take out

extraordinary unusual, out of the ordinary

extravagant spending too much money

extreme very great, more than usual

eye the part of the body one sees with

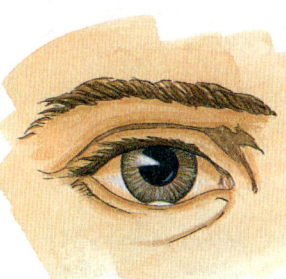

eyebrow a line of hairs above the eye socket

eyelash hairs on the lid that protect the eye

eyrie the nest of a bird of prey

DICTIONARY 51

F

fable a short story, often about animals, with a moral (fabulous)

fabric cloth

face the front of the head where the eyes, nose and mouth are

fact something that has happened or been done, something that is true

factory a place where goods are made by machine

fade to get lighter in colour, or die away

fail to be unsuccessful (failure)

faint 1. to lose consciousness: *Many people fainted in the heat.*
2. weak, not strong: *Roger drew a faint line on the paper.*

fair 1. light coloured: *Ruth had fair hair and blue eyes.*
2. just, doing what is right: *The teacher was always very fair.*
3. a place where goods are sold and there are amusements such as merry-go-rounds: *Janet and John went to a fair last week.*

fairy a small imaginary person with wings

fall/fell to drop down by accident, to collapse

false untrue, wrong, disloyal (falsehood)

fame to be well known and well spoken of (famous)

familiar well known, on easy terms with

family a group of persons who are related and live together

famine a great shortage of food

famished starving, very hungry

fancy 1. a liking for: *Tom had a fancy for dark chocolate.*
2. to believe without proof (fanciful): *I fancy you know the way to my house.*
3. very ornamental: *Brenda wore a fancy dress to the party.*

52 DICTIONARY

fang the long sharp tooth of a dog, wolf or snake

fantastic very strange, amazing

far a long way away

fare 1. the price paid for a journey by bus, train, etc.
2. food: *The fare at the hotel was very good.*
3. to get on: *How did you fare in your exams?*

farm a place where crops are grown or animals reared (farmer)

fascinate to charm and interest very much (fascination)

fashion 1. to make: *Roy fashioned a stick into an arrow.*
2. the style in which something is made or done (fashionable): *Jeans are very much in fashion these days.*

fast 1. able to go at speed (a fast car)
2. to stop eating all or certain foods for a time

fasten to close and make secure (zip fastener)

fatal causing death or disaster

fate whatever is bound to happen

father a male parent

fault a mistake or error

favour 1. kindness or goodwill (favourite): *As a favour, the teacher gave the class a day off.*
2. to prefer or help: *Jim favours going to the seaside tomorrow.*

fawn 1. a light brown colour
2. a young deer
3. to flatter someone and curry favour: *The dog fawned upon its master.*

fear to be afraid of

feast to eat and drink large amounts (feasting)

feather the covering on the body of a bird

February the second month of the year

fee payment for special work or services

feeble weak

feed/fed to give food to

F

feel/felt to find out by touch, have a sensation (feeling)

feign to pretend

female of the sex that can bear young

fence 1. a rail around a piece of land (fencing) 2. to fight with swords (fencer)

ferocious very fierce and savage

ferret a small animal that chases rats and rabbits out of their holes

ferry a boat that carries passengers across a short stretch of water

fertile able to grow crops (fertility)

festival a feast or celebration for a particular event

fetch to go and bring something or someone

fête a festival or fair arranged to raise funds

feud a bitter quarrel that goes on for a long time between two people or families

fever an illness where the sick person has a high temperature (feverish)

few not many

fiancé a person engaged to be married

fiction a story which is not true

fidget to move restlessly

field a space of ground where crops are grown

fiend an evil spirit

fierce cruel, savage, ferocious

fiery made of fire and flames

fight/fought to wage war or struggle against an enemy (fighter)

figure 1. a number or amount (the figure 7) 2. the shape of a body

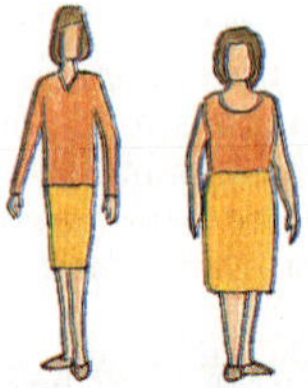

3. a diagram or drawing

file 1. a steel tool with a rough surface that is used to make things smooth by rubbing: *The carpenter smoothed the wood with his file.*
2. a row of people (single file)
3. a pocket or container for holding papers, photographs etc.: *Jean put all the letters in a file.*

54 DICTIONARY

F

fill to put something into a container, to make full

film 1. a roll of flexible plastic used in taking photographs: *David put a new film in the camera.*
2. a thing covering on the surface: *The puddle was covered by a thin film of oil.*

filth dirt, pollution (filthy)

fin the part of a fish like a small wing that it uses to balance and swim

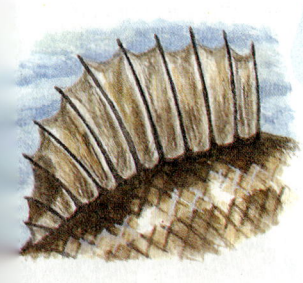

final the last part or end

find/found to discover by searching or by accident

fine 1. delicate, thin: *The brooch was made of fine wires.*
2. to make someone pay money as a punishment: *The burglar was fined a large sum.*

finger a part of the body at the end of the hand

finish to bring to an end

fir a kind of tree with long thin leaves that bears cones

fire a means of heating by burning

firework a container which explodes and makes pretty patterns of sparkling stars, etc.

firm 1. strong and steady: *The tree was firm in the ground.*
2. a business organisation: *Wendy's firm makes plastic containers.*

fish to catch creatures that live in water

fist a hand where the fingers are curled up or clenched

fix to arrange or make firm (fixture)

fizz to make a hissing bubbling sound

flabby soft and loose

DICTIONARY 55

F

flag 1. a cloth with a design that stands for a country or association: *The Olympic flag is international.*

2. to droop or hang loosely: *Peter was flagging after his long walk.*

flake to make small light particles or scales

flame a hot, bright body of burning gas

flare to burn with a glaring unsteady flame

flash a short, sudden blaze of light

flask a small bottle with a narrow neck

flap to move rapidly up and down

flat 1. very even and smooth
2. an apartment in a building

flatter to praise without being sincere; to pretend admiration

flavour to add taste to food

flaw a fault or weak point

flea a small jumping insect that bites animals and humans

flee to run away as quickly as possible

fleece the wool of a sheep

fleet a group of ships, aircraft, cars etc.

flexible able to bend easily

flicker a short unsteady wavering gleam of light

flimsy weak and not well made

fling to throw from the hand

flint a very hard kind of stone

flit to fly away or dart along

float 1. to rest on the surface of the water
2. a decorated lorry in a procession

flock a group of birds or animals

flog to beat with a stick (flogging)

flood to overflow with water

56 DICTIONARY

floor the flat surface of a room on which one walks

florist a shopkeeper who sells flowers

flour a powder made from grinding up wheat

flourish to grow well

flow to move like a stream of liquid

flower to bloom or produce blossom

flue a pipe through which smoke passes from a fireplace

fluent able to speak easily and smoothly

fluid liquid which can flow as water does

flush to blush and get red in the face

fluster to get worried and anxious

flute an instrument that you blow to make music

flutter to flap the wings (fluttering)

fly/flew 1. to move through the sky (flight) 2. an insect with wings

foal a baby horse

foam froth or bubbles

foe an enemy

foil 1. to prevent a person from doing things: *The man foiled the thief's attempt to steal his car.* 2. a thin metal wrapping that keeps food fresh

fold to bend over and make a crease or a line

foliage the leaves on a tree or a plant

folk people

follow to go after or behind somebody (follower, following)

folly a foolish action

fond to like a person, loving

food matter that one eats

fool 1. a silly person (foolish) 2. to deceive: *Jim was fooled by the sign on the door.*

foot part of the body at the end of your leg that you use to walk with (feet)

F

football a game played with a blown up leather ball between two teams (footballer)

footlights the lights at floor level along the front of a stage

footpath a narrow path for walkers or pedestrians

footstep the sound of someone walking

forbid/forbade to order a person not to do something

force 1. to use strength: *James forced the door open by pushing hard.* 2. to make a person do something: *Joy forced herself to eat the pudding.*

ford to cross a shallow area in a river

forearm the part of the arm between the elbow and the wrist

forecast to tell beforehand

forefather one of your ancestors

forehead the upper part of the face above the nose

foreign from another country (foreigner)

forest an area of land covered with trees

forfeit to have something taken away because of your own fault

forge 1. to beat into shape by heating and hammering 2. where a blacksmith works and has a fire

forget/forgot not to remember, to overlook (forgetfulness)

forgive/forgave to no longer be angry with someone (forgiveness)

fork 1. a tool or instrument with prongs at the end 2. to divide in two: *After the corner the road forks.*

form 1. to shape or make: *Ellen formed a house from the lump of clay.* 2. a class: *The whole form went into the hall.* 3. a printed piece of paper: *Ted had to fill in lots of forms after his accident.*

58 DICTIONARY

F

formal according to a fixed way of doing things, not casual

former earlier, having happened before

forsake/forsook to leave a place or person, to abandon

fort a strongly built building to keep enemies out

fortify to make stronger from attack (fortification)

fortnight two weeks together

fortune good luck, or a large amount of money (fortunate)

forward towards the front

foster to take care of another person's children

foul 1. nasty, dirty 2. to do something not according to the rules: *The referee called a foul when one player kicked another.*

fountain a spout or jet of water coming up from a pipe and falling into a basin

fowl a farmyard bird

fox a wild animal like a dog that lives underground

fraction a small part, a portion

fracture to break something

fragile delicate and easily broken

fragment a portion or part that has broken off

fragrant sweet smelling

frail not at all strong

frame to put a border around a picture

frantic very worried and anxious

fraud to deceive or trick someone

freak odd or not natural

freckle a small brown spot just under the skin

F

free 1. to be loose, not tied down (freedom): *The dog broke free from his leash.* 2. not costing anything, with nothing to pay: *The driver gave us a free ride on his bus.*

freeze/froze cold enough to turn water into ice

frenzy madness or very frantic

frequent happening often

fresh new, recently made, not stale

friction rubbing one thing against another

Friday the sixth day of the week

fridge a cold cupboard for storing food to keep it fresh

friend a person you like very much and get on with (friendly)

frighten to make afraid, to scare (fright)

fringe 1. the outside edge of something: *Joe stood on the fringe of the crowd to watch the game.* 2. a border made of threads that hangs down 3. hair hanging over the forehead

frisky jumping and skipping about

frock a dress

frog a small animal with webbed feet that lives both on land and in water

front the opposite of back, the forepart

frontier the border between two countries

frost very cold weather when the water in the air turns to ice

froth to make a collection of small bubbles on the surface

frown to show displeasure by drawing down the eyebrows

fruit the part of a plant around the seed

fry/fried to cook in hot oil or fat

fuel material for burning, such as coal or wood

fugitive a person who runs away from danger

full filled to the top

fumes gases or smoke that smell bitter

fund a supply of money kept for a special purpose

60 DICTIONARY

funeral the ceremony when a dead person is buried

fungus a plant that cannot make its own food from sunlight

funnel 1. a cone with a tube for filling objects with narrow necks: *Anne poured the juice into the bottle through a funnel.* 2. a large chimney on a boat

funny amusing, making one laugh

fur the hair on the body of an animal

furious very angry

furnace a fire burning inside a closed fireplace

furnish to put tables, chairs, beds etc. inside a house (furniture)

furtive secret, sly, stealthy

fuss to worry and bother about little things that are not important

future the time that is coming or about to happen

G

gadget a useful tool or implement

gain to obtain more

gale a very strong wind

gallery 1. a building in which works of art are on show (art gallery) 2. a long corridor, hall or room

galley 1. the kitchen in a ship or plane 2. a kind of open ship rowed by oars in ancient times

gamble to play games of chance for money (gambler)

game 1. an amusement or children's play: *John and Ted like to play football.* 2. wild animals or birds that are hunted for sport

DICTIONARY 61

G

gander a male goose

gang a group of people who do things together (gangster)

gangway the steps leading from the dockside to the deck of a ship

gaol a prison

gape to stare with the mouth open

garage a building for a car, or where a car is repaired

garden a piece of ground near a house for growing flowers and vegetables (gardener)

gargle to rinse the throat with liquid which one does not swallow

garlic a strong smelling plant used to flavour food

gas an invisible substance that is not liquid or solid

gash to cut deeply

gasp to struggle for breath

gate a barred frame that shuts off an opening in a fence or wall

gather 1. to come or bring together (gathering): *The crowd gathered outside the town hall.*
2. to pick: *Ellen gathered some flowers for her mother.*

gaze to look at for a long time

gazelle a kind of small deer

gear a wheel or lever used to change the speed of a machine or engine

gem a precious stone or jewel

general 1. an important officer in the army
2. for everybody, not for only a few

generation people of the same age who live at the same time

generous willing to giving freely, kind–hearted

genie a kind of spirit

genius a very clever person

62 DICTIONARY

G

gentle not rough or cruel; kind and pleasant (gentleness, gentleman)

genuine real, not a copy of something

geography the study of the earth and its mountains, rivers and seas

germ a tiny living substance that can cause disease

ghastly horrible, dreadful

ghost the spirit of a dead person

giant a very, very tall person

giddy feeling dizzy, with a whirling feeling in the head

give to hand over (gift)

gigantic very large, enormous

giggle to laugh in a silly way

gild to cover with gold

gill the flap on the side of a fish which opens and shuts when it breathes

ginger 1. a root with a hot, sharp taste used to flavour food
2. a reddish brown colour

gipsy a traveller who lives in a caravan instead of a house

giraffe an animal with a very long neck and long legs

girl a female child

give/gave to make a present of, to hand over

glacier a slow moving river of ice

glad pleased and happy

glade an open space inside a wood or forest

glance to look at quickly

glare 1. to stare angrily: *The man glared at the naughty boys.*
2. a very bright light that dazzles

glass 1. a hard brittle material that can often be seen through
2. a drinking vessel

glasses spectacles

gleam to shine brightly

glee joy

DICTIONARY 63

G

glen a narrow valley in the mountains

glide to move easily and smoothly

glider a plane with no engine that floats on currents of air

glimmer to shine faintly

glimpse to see for only a short time

glisten to shine

glitter to sparkle with light

globe a round ball

gloom darkness or unhappiness

glory honour and fame

glossy shiny

glove a covering to keep the hand warm

glow to shine with a warm steady light

glue to join two things together with a sticky substance

gnarled twisted and bent over

gnash to grind one's teeth in rage

gnat a small insect that bites

gnaw to scrape away with the teeth

goal 1. the posts on a playing field where the ball must go (goalkeeper) 2. an aim or ambition: *David's goal was to be a pilot.*

goat a small to medium domestic animal with long hair and short horns that gives milk

gobble to eat very quickly

goblin a kind of fairy

gold a precious yellow metal found in the earth

goldfish a small fish with gold–coloured scales

golf a game played with a small ball and long sticks called clubs

goose a large web–footed bird (geese)

gooseberry a hard green fruit with a hairy skin

64 DICTIONARY

gorge 1. to eat greedily: *Jennifer gorged herself on strawberries and cream.*
2. a narrow passage between high cliffs

gorgeous splendid, magnificent

gorilla a large, hairy ape

gorse a prickly bush with yellow flowers

gossamer made of fine threads like cobwebs

gossip to chat about things that are not important

govern to rule over people (governor, government)

gown a long, loose dress

grab to snatch or take quickly

grace 1. beauty of appearance and movement (graceful): *Wendy's dancing was full of grace.*
2. a short prayer said before meals

gradual going slowly by small steps

grain 1. the seeds of corn, wheat, barley, etc.
2. a small hard particle (a grain of salt)
3. the direction of the fibres in wood

granary a place for storing grain

grand great, important

granite a very hard kind of rock

granule a little grain, a small particle

grape the sweet, juicy fruit of a vine

grapefruit a round, yellow citrus fruit

grasp to seize or hold firmly

grass plants that grow on a lawn or in fields and are eaten by animals such as cows

grasshopper an chirping insect that lives in grass

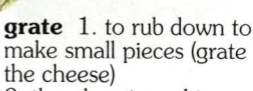

grate 1. to rub down to make small pieces (grate the cheese)
2. the place in a chimney where the fire burns

grateful thankful for kindness

G

grave a hole in the ground where a dead body is placed

gravel small stones on a drive or path

gravy a sauce made from the juices of the meat

graze to eat grass

grease (say grees) melted animal fat, or very thick oil (greasy)

grease (say greeze) to put on thick oil to stop anything rubbing together

great important, large in size or number

greed very fond of eating (greedy)

green a colour made by mixing blue and yellow

greengrocer a person who sells fruit and vegetables

greenhouse a glass house to keep plants warm

greet to welcome or receive (greeting)

grey a colour between black and white

grieve to feel sad, sorrow (grief)

grim stern, unfriendly

grime dirt

grin to smile widely

grind/ground to crush into powder

grip to hold on tightly

gristle a tough material between the joints (gristly)

grit dust, gravel or bits of stone

grizzly a bear that lives in North America

groan to moan in pain

grocer a person who sells food

groom to brush down a horse

groove a line cut out of the surrounding material

grope to feel one's way in the dark

ground the surface of the earth

group a collection of people or things that are alike in some way

grouse 1. a wild game bird

2. to grumble or complain

grow/grew to get larger or develop (growth)

growl a low warning sound made in the throat by a dog

grub the stage of life in an insect before it becomes an adult

grudge to feel angry, jealous or resentful

gruff having a rough voice or manner

grumble to complain about

grunt to make a noise like a pig

guerilla a member of an armed band of troops who are not regular soldiers

guard to protect or watch over (guardian)

guess to estimate or think without a basis in fact

guest a visitor or friend who stays in your house

guide to show the way or give advice

guilt the state of having committed a crime (guilty)

guinea pig a small animal that has long front teeth for gnawing

guitar a hollow musical instrument with strings that the player strums

gulf a large bay running far inland

gull a large seabird

gulp to swallow a drink quickly and noisily

gurgle to make a bubbling sound

gush to flow out very fast

gust a sudden rush of wind

gutter a passage for water to escape

gymnasium a building with equipment for physical training

H

habit to do something in the same way every time

hack to cut up roughly and carelessly

H

haddock a sea fish of the cod family

hail 1. to call out or greet: *John hailed his friend from a distance.* 2. frozen rain

hair natural, fine threads that grow on your head

hairdresser a person who cuts and washes hair

hall a long passage between rooms in a building

hallmark a mark stamped on gold or silver as a sign of good quality

halo a circle of light around the head of a saint or angel

halt to stop moving

halter a rope to lead a horse

halve to cut into two equal parts (half, halves)

hamburger a flat cake of beef served in a bread roll

hammer to beat on or knock nails into

hammock a hanging bed tied by ropes at each end

hamper 1. to make it difficult to do something: *The driver was hampered by faulty brakes.*
2. a large basket with a lid

hamster a kind of rat with large cheeks where it stores food

hand 1. the end of the arm beyond the wrist 2. cards dealt to one of the players in a game

handcuff to put a pair of steel rings joined by a chain onto the wrists of a prisoner

handicap to prevent a person doing the best they can

handkerchief a piece of cloth to wipe the nose

handle 1. the part of an article which one holds in the hand
2. to touch or feel: *Kittens and puppies should be handled with care.*

68 DICTIONARY

H

handsome good looking

handy convenient or useful

hang to fasten at the top so the rest of the article drops or falls downwards

hang glider a glider where the flier hangs below the wings

hangar a building where aeroplanes are kept

happen to take place or occur (happening)

happy contented, joyful

harbour a shelter for ships

harden to make solid, not soft or yielding

hare a wild animal like a rabbit with long back legs

harm to hurt or cause injury

harness to put leather straps on a horse before it is ridden or fastened to a cart or carriage

harp a large stringed instrument which is played by plucking the strings

harpoon a spear with hooks on it and a rope attached to catch fish

harsh rough and unfeeling

harvest to gather in the crops when they are ripe

hasten to hurry (make haste)

hatch 1. to break the shell and come out of an egg: *The chicks hatched out of the eggs.* 2. a small wooden door 3. to make a plan or plot

hatchet a small axe with a long handle

hate to dislike very much, to detest

haughty proud

haul to pull hard or drag

haunt to visit very often, like a ghost

hawk a small bird of prey

hay dry grass used as food for animals in winter

DICTIONARY 69

H

haze a misty appearance in the air

hazel a tree which has small sweet nuts

head to upper part of the body

headache a pain in the head

headland a piece of land that juts out into the sea

headlight one of the main lights on the front of a car

headquarters the centre of a battlefield or where the officers live

heal to make well (healing)

health when one is well and has no sickness (healthy)

heap to pile up

hear to listen or receive sounds through the ear (hearer, hearing)

heart the organ inside the chest that pumps blood around the body

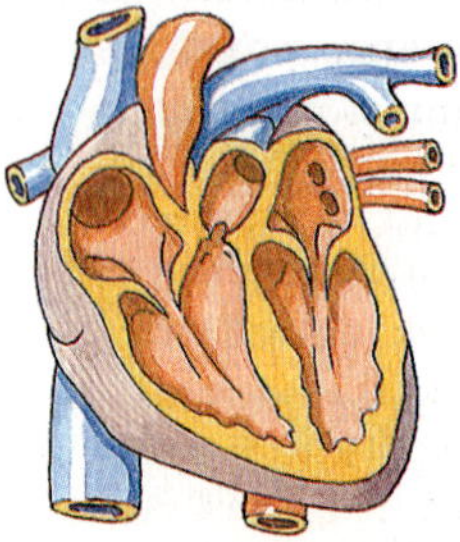

hearth a fireplace

heat 1. to make warm or hot (heater, heating): *Ben heated up some soup for his father.* 2. an early part of a race to find out who will be in the final race

heath an area of waste land with grass and shrubs

heathen a person who does not believe in a religion

heather a low growing plant with purple flowers and tough stems

heave to lift and throw

heaven a place of great happiness, the sky

heavy difficult to lift or move, not light

hedge a line of bushes by the side of a field

hedgehog an animal with many prickly quills

heed to pay attention to

heel the back part of the foot

heifer a young cow

height the measurement from the bottom to the top

heir a person who gets the possessions of someone who has died

70 DICTIONARY

H

heirloom an article that has been in the same family for many generations

helicopter a flying machine with whirling blades which can rise straight up in the air and come straight down

helm to steer a ship

helmet a metal covering to protect the head from injury

help to aid or assist, to be useful (helper)

helping the portion of food one is given on a plate

hemisphere half a globe

herald a person who makes an announcement

herb any plant used to flavour food or as a medicine

herd to group animals together

hermit a person who lives alone and tries not to meet other people

hero a person who has done something very brave (heroine)

herring a small sea fish caught for food

hesitate to hold back from doing something (hesitation)

hew to cut or chop with an axe

hibernate to go to sleep during the winter (hibernation)

hide/hid 1. to keep out of sight: *The children hid in the shed.* 2. the skin of a large animal

hideous very ugly

high far up, not low, tall (height)

highway a main road

hilarious very funny

hill a small mountain or fold in the ground

hinder to stop or prevent from doing something (hindrance)

hinge a movable joint or fastening

hint to suggest in a roundabout way

DICTIONARY 71

H

hippopotamus a very large African animal with a wide mouth which lives in rivers and on land

hire to pay for using something for a time

hiss to make a sss sound like a snake does to show disapproval

history the story of what has happened in the past

hitch 1. to tie up or fasten to something: *Ruth hitched the reins to the gate post.* 2. a problem or snag: *There was a hitch in the arrangements for the concert.*

hive a place where bees live

hoarse rough and harsh sounding

hoax to play a trick on someone

hobble to walk with a limp

hobby what one likes to do in one's spare time

hockey a game that is played with curved sticks and a ball

hoist to raise or lift up

hold/held 1. to grasp and keep fast, to cling to, to contain (holder): *The drowning man held on to the piece of wood.* 2. the space below the deck of a ship where the cargo is stored

hole an opening

holiday a time of rest from work or school

hollow to make something empty inside

holly a prickly evergreen bush with red berries

holy sacred, to do with God

home the place where one lives

honesty worthy of trust, never lying or stealing

honey a sweet, sugary liquid made by bees from nectar

honeycomb the wax cells in which bees store honey

72 DICTIONARY

H

honour to show respect and value for someone's good name

hood a cloth covering for the head

hoof the hard, horny part of the feet of animals such as deer and cattle (hooves)

hook to catch with a piece of curved metal

hoot to make a sound like that of an owl or the horn of a car

hope to wish and believe that something will happen

horizon the line where the sky and the earth seem to meet in the distance (horizontal)

horn 1. the pointed bony growths on the heads of deer and cattle
2. a musical instrument made of brass

hornet a kind of large wasp with a bad sting

horror fear and dread (horrible)

horse a large animal with hoofs used for riding

hose 1. a long flexible pipe or tube
2. stockings

hospital a building where sick people are cared for by doctors and nurses

host 1. a large number: *A host of friends came to Jane's party.*
2. a person who entertains another (hostess): *The door was opened by our host.*

hostage a person handed over to the enemy to be sure that a promise will be kept

hostility an unfriendly act (hostile)

hotel a place where travellers can stay

hound a dog bred for hunting

hour a unit of time

house a place where people live

hovel a hut or small, dirty house

DICTIONARY 73

H

hover to hang with wings beating above one spot

hovercraft a machine which skims over the water just above the waves

howl to give a long, loud cry of distress

hub the centre of a wheel

huddle to crowd close together

hue 1. the shade or colour: *The dress was all the hues of the rainbow.*
2. a loud shouting or noise: *The theft of the cup caused a loud hue and cry.*

hullo see hello

human belonging to people, not animals

humble meek and modest, not proud

humour 1. to put in a good frame of mind: *Jill decided to humour her grandfather and fetch his pipe.*
2. fun or good temper (humorous): *The audience enjoyed the humour of the play.*

hump a lump on the back

hunchback a person with a twisted back

hunger a strong need or desire for food (hungry)

hunt to chase and kill an animal (hunter)

hurdle to jump over a frame of twigs or wooden bars

hurl to throw away with great force

hurricane a very strong wind storm

hurry to move quickly

hurt to wound or cause pain

husband a married man

hush to make quiet

hutch a small wooden cage for an rabbit

hyacinth a sweet-smelling spring flower with all the flowers on one stem

hyena a wild dog like animal that hunts other animals in a pack

74 **DICTIONARY**

hymn a song of praise

hypocrite a person who pretends to be good and kind without real cause

I

ice 1. frozen water (icy) 2. to cover a cake with a mixture of sugar and water (icing)

iceberg a huge mass of floating ice

icicle a long thin piece of ice made from drips of water that freeze

idea a thought or mental picture

ideal the best that can be imagined, perfect

identical exactly the same

identify to recognise and know a person or thing (identity)

idiot a fool who cannot think clearly (idiotic)

idle lazy, not at work (idleness)

idol a figure of a person or animal worshipped as a god

ignorant having no knowledge of

ignore to pay no attention to (ignorance)

ill unwell, sick

illegal against the law

illegible unable to be read

illuminate to light up (illumination)

illustrate to make a picture or drawing (illustration)

imagine to picture in the mind (imagination)

imitate to copy (imitation)

immature not fully grown or mature

immediate without any delay

immense very large

impassable where the road or route is blocked

impatient in a hurry, not patient

imperfect not perfect

impertinent cheeky, rude

implement a tool or instrument for doing some work

DICTIONARY 75

I

implore to beg or plead

impolite not polite

import to bring goods into a country from another country

important necessary and of great weight

impostor a person who pretends to be another

impress to make a mark or figure upon, to fix in the mind (impression)

improve to make something better (improvement)

impudent rude, cheeky

impulse a sudden idea

incessant endless, without ceasing

include to take in or contain (inclusion)

income the money that a person earns or gets

increase to make or get larger

incurable not able to be cured

indelible leaving marks that cannot be removed

independent free, not influenced by others (independence)

index an alphabetical list of subjects and their page numbers at the back of a book

indicate to show or point out (indication)

indigestion having pain and discomfort because one cannot digest food

indignation angry because of a wrong doing (indignant)

individual a single person, animal or thing

industry 1. a liking for work (industrious): *Peter showed great industry in cleaning his car.* 2. trade or manufacture (industrial): *The steel industry makes a lot of money.*

inevitable cannot be avoided, certain to take place

inexhaustible not able to be exhausted or emptied

inexperienced not trained and with no experience

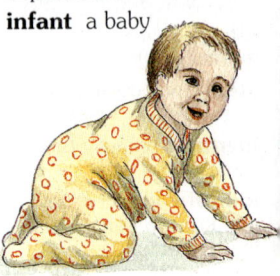

infant a baby

infect to pass on a disease

inferior lower in quality or rank

infinite without any limit or end

76 DICTIONARY

I

infirm unwell, not strong

inflamed red and sore

inflate to put air inside or blow up (inflation)

inflict to punish or penalize (infliction)

influence to have an effect upon

inform to tell about (informant, information)

informal not formal, free and easy

infuriate to make very angry

ingenious clever in thinking up new ideas or ways of doing things

ingredient one part of a mixture

inhabit to live in (inhabitant)

inhale to suck in air (inhalation)

inherit to receive money or goods as an heir (inheritance)

initial 1. the first letter of a name: *Bill wrote his initials on his exercise book.*

2. occurring at the beginning: *My initial thought was that Julie was not coming.*

inject to force into (injection)

injure to cause harm (injury)

inland away from the seaside, in the country

innocent not guilty

innumerable too many to be counted

inquire to ask about (inquiry)

inscribe to write upon (inscription)

insect a tiny six-legged animal

insert to put into (insertion)

DICTIONARY 77

I

insist to ask or demand and refuse to give way (insistence)

inspect to look at very carefully (inspector, inspection)

install to put in place (installation)

instance an example

instant a very short moment of time

instead in place of

instinct an inner feeling of what to do without thinking about it

instruct to teach or give orders to (instruction)

instrument a tool or thing that is used to do a piece of work or produce musical sounds

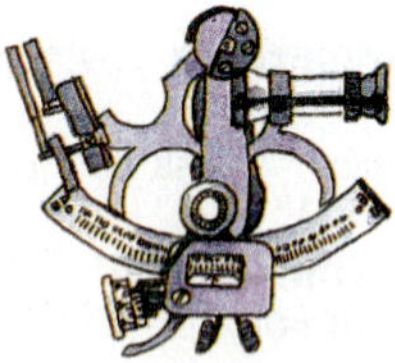

insult to make a rude remark about someone

intelligence the power of understanding (intelligent)

intend to mean or aim to (intention)

intense very strong

interest to pay keen attention

interfere to meddle in the affairs of others (interference)

interior inside

internal the inner side

international happening between two or more nations or countries

interpret to explain or make a meaning clear (interpretation)

interrupt to stop or break in on (interruption)

interval the space between two things or the time between

interview a discussion between two people about a particular subject

intrigue a secret plot (intriguing)

introduce to make one person known to another (introduction)

intrude to go where one is not wanted (intrusion)

invade to enter a country by force (invasion)

invalid (say inv_a_lid) having lost its value: *Jane found that her bus ticket was invalid because it was out of date.*

invalid (say _i_nvaleed) a sick person

invent to think out something quite new (invention)

investigate to explore or examine carefully (investigation)

invite to ask to come to a place or event (invitation)

irate angry

iron a strong metal found in the earth

irregular not regular or even

irritate to annoy or make cross (irritation)

island a piece of land surrounded by water

issue to give or send out

italic a printed letter that slopes forwards

item a single article on a list

ivory a hard white material which comes from the tusks of elephants

ivy a climbing plant which grows on walls and trees

jack a machine for lifting up heavy weights, especially cars

jackal a wild animal like a dog, with a bushy tail, found in Africa and Asia

jacket a short coat

jade a hard, green stone which is carved and polished to make ornaments

jagged having rough edges and sharp points

jail a prison

jangle to make an unpleasant ringing sound

January the first month of the year

jaunt a pleasant outing or journey

jaw the bones of the mouth that support the teeth

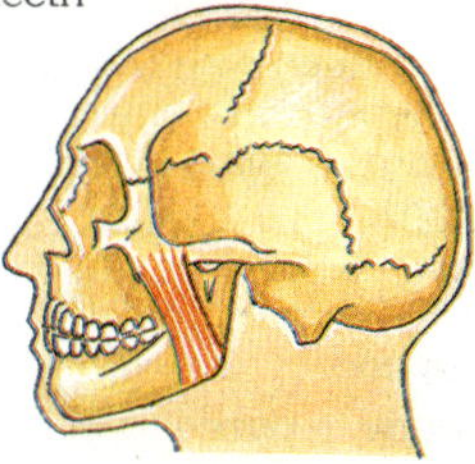

DICTIONARY 79

J

jealousy envy of someone for something you would like to have (jealous)

jeans trousers made from a strong cloth, usually blue in colour

jeep a small, light military vehicle

jeer to laugh at or make fun of in an unkind way

jellyfish an animal that lives in the sea and looks like a lump of jelly floating in the water

jerk to make a sudden sharp movement

jest to make a joke (jester)

jet 1. a plane with engines that suck in air at the front and push it out in a hot stream behind them
2. a sudden rush of liquid or flame from a small pipe or opening (a jet of water)

jewel a precious stone, such as a ruby or diamond

jigsaw a puzzle where each part locks into the pieces beside it

jockey the rider of a racehorse

jog 1. to push with the hand or elbow: *Tim spilt the juice when his brother jogged his arm.* 2. to run at a steady pace: *Anna jogged around the park every morning.*

join to bring or fasten together (junction)

joint 1. where two things meet and are joined, especially in the body (elbow joint, knee joint)
2. a piece of meat

joke to say or do something that makes people laugh

jolly merry and cheerful

jolt to shake with a sudden jerk

journalist someone whose work is to write for newspapers and magazines (journalism)

journey to make a trip or travel from one place to another

80 DICTIONARY

K

joy a feeling of gladness or happiness (joyful)

jubilee a festival or time of celebration and rejoicing

judge to decide whether something is good or bad (judgment)

juggle to do conjuring tricks with balls or other objects (juggler)

juice the liquid from fruit or vegetables (juicy)

July the seventh month of the year

jumble to mix together in an untidy pile

jump to leap up, or spring over something

June the sixth month of the year

jungle a thick forest of tropical trees and plants

junior a younger person

junk 1. a Chinese sailing vessel

2. useless bits and pieces of things

jury people in a court of law who hear the evidence and decide together on the verdict

just 1. fair, lawful, correct (justice): *The thief knew that his punishment was just.* 2. exactly, barely: *There were just enough sweets for everybody.*

K

kaleidoscope a tube with mirrors and coloured pieces of glass that make different patterns when the tube is shaken

kangaroo an animal with strong back legs for jumping. The female carries her babies in a pouch.

keel the long, strong beam which is the lowest part of the ship

DICTIONARY 81

K

keen eager, sharp, interested

keep/kept to maintain in good order; to guard and not lose something (keeper)

kennel a small house for a dog

kernel the inside part of a nut or fruit-stone

kettle a metal container with a spout and a handle used to boil water

key a tool to open or close a lock

khaki a yellowish brown colour

kick to strike with the foot

kidnap to carry off a person against their will

kidney the part of the body where the blood is cleaned of waste products

kill to take the life of (killer)

kiln a large closed oven used for drying or baking pots

kilt a pleated skirt made of tartan cloth worn by Scots people

kind 1. a sort, class or variety of something: *Oranges, lemons and grapefruits are different kinds of citrus fruits.* 2. sympathetic and helpful (kindness): *Nora's friend was very kind to her.*

kindergarten a school for very young children

king a man who rules over a country and its people (kingdom)

kingfisher a bird with blue wing and tail feathers that lives near rivers

kiosk a stall or stand to sell sweets or tobacco

82 DICTIONARY

kiss to touch with the lips as an expression of love and affection

kitchen a room where food is prepared and cooked

kite 1. a sheet of light material such as paper or plastic stretched over a frame and flown in the wind by a string or cord fastened to it
2. a bird of prey

kitten a baby cat

knave a dishonest person

knead to work up flour into a dough by squeezing it with the hands

knee the joint between the upper and lower part of the leg

kneel/knelt to rest on the knees

knife a tool with a sharp blade fastened to a handle used for cutting (knives)

knight a British title given by the Queen that allows him to use Sir instead of Mr in front of his name

knit to make something such as a sweater using wool and long needles

knob a small, hard, round lump at the end or on the surface of something

knock to strike or beat with something hard or heavy (knocker)

knot to twist cords or threads so they fasten together

know/knew to have information about or recognize (knowledge)

knuckle the bony joints in the fingers

koala an Australian bear that lives in trees

DICTIONARY 83

L

label to fasten a slip of paper onto something, giving its contents or destination

laboratory a place used for scientific research and experiments

labour to work hard (labourer)

lack to want or need

ladder a frame of wood, steel or ropes with bars between which act as steps

ladle to put soup onto plates with a long spoon

lady a formal, polite name for a woman

ladybird a small flying insect with a red back and black spots

lagoon a shallow lake connected with the sea or a river

lair the home or bed of a wild animal

lake a large piece of water with land all around it

lamb a baby sheep

lame unable to walk properly because of an injury to a leg or foot

lamp a vessel which burns fuel to make light

land the part of the earth not covered by the sea

landlord a person who owns land or houses (landlady)

lane a narrow country road

language the words and speech of a nation

lantern a lamp that can be carried about or hung

larch a kind of conifer that loses its leaves in winter

larder a small room to store food

large very big

larva a stage in the life of an insect between the egg and the adult

lash 1. to strike with a whip: *The rider lashed his horse to make it gallop faster.*
2. to tie together: *Penny lashed the logs of wood together to make a raft.*

84 DICTIONARY

L

lasso to catch horses or cattle in a noose at the end of a rope

last 1. after all the others: *Billy was the last one to enter the classroom.*
2. to continue or hold out: *The paint lasted for a long time.*

late after the usual or expected time

lather froth made by soap bubbles in water

latitude the distance either north or south of the equator

laugh to make a noise to show amusement (laughter)

launch to move a boat into the sea

laundry a place where clothes are washed

lava hot ash and rocks thrown out by a volcano

lavender a sweet smelling blue grey flower

law the rules made by the government of a country (lawyer)

lawn the grassy part of a garden

lay/laid to spread out or put down on something (layer)

lazy unwilling to work or be active

lead (say led) a soft bluish grey metal used for roofing and pipes

lead/led (say leed) to guide or go before (leader)

leaf the flat green blade growing from the stem or branch of a plant or tree (leaves)

leaflet a small printed notice

leak to let water escape

lean/leant 1. to rest weight against: *James leant against the wall.*
2. to bend forward: *Erica leaned over the tank of fish.*
3. without any fat: *Mark would only eat lean meat.*

DICTIONARY 85

L

leap/leapt to jump over

learn to study and get knowledge or experience (learning)

leash a strap or chain to hold a dog

leather the skin of an animal after the hair or wool has been removed

leave/left 1. to go away from a place: *Bill left London and went to Bath.*
2. allow to remain: *Leave the glass on the table.*
3. to have a holiday from work: *James spent all his leave fishing.*

lecture a talk or speech on a particular subject

ledge a narrow shelf from a wall or cliff

leek a long, white vegetable with a flavour like an onion

left connected with the side of the body on which the heart is

legend a traditional old story

legible easy to read

leisure time free from work

lemon a yellow citrus fruit with an acid flavour

lemonade a sweet drink made from the juice of lemons

lend/lent to let a person have something for a time on condition it is returned (loan)

lengthen to make longer (length)

leopard a large fierce cat–like animal with a brown spotted coat

lesson a period of teaching time

letter 1. one of the 26 symbols of the alphabet
2. a written message sent by post: *Mary wrote a letter to her brother in Australia.*

lettuce a leafy, green salad plant

level to give something a flat surface

library a building or room containing a collection of books (librarian)

licence to give permission to do something, such as keep a dog

lick to pass the tongue over

lie 1. to say something that is not true (liar): *Mary lied about her age.*
2. to rest on something or stretch out: *Peter lay down to rest on his bed.*

lieutenant a junior officer in the army or navy

lifebuoy a belt made of rubber or cork which can support a person in the water

lift 1. to raise up: *Dave lifted up the heavy branch.*
2. a small cage or room that carries people between different floors in a building: *Jenny took the lift to the top floor of the hotel.*

light/lit 1. to use the energy from the sun to make things visible: *The rays of the sun lit up the room.*
2. to set fire to: *The twins lit the fire to warm themselves up.*
3. not heavy: *The basket was light and easy to carry.*

lighthouse a high tower with a light at the top to warn ships of dangerous rocks

lightning a flash of electricity during a thunderstorm

like 1. to enjoy or be pleased with: *Ben likes reading but James prefers sports.*
2. equal or similar: *That dog looks like a collie.*

lilac a sweet smelling, pale mauve flower that grows as a shrub

DICTIONARY 87

L

lily a sweet smelling flower that grows from a bulb

limb an arm or leg, or the branch of a tree

lime a green citrus fruit that tastes like a lemon

limit to keep within a boundary or set of rules

limp 1. to walk as if lame: *Jean walked with a limp after her accident.*
2. not stiff or hard: Some books have limp covers.

line 1. a string or wire stretched between two points: *Meg hung the washing outside on the line.*
2. a thin mark between two points: *Martin drew a line across the paper.*

linen cloth made from flax

linger to delay or go very slowly

lion a large, fierce wild African animal like a cat, the male of which has long hair on its head and neck

liquid not solid, but able to flow

listen to pay attention to noises or sounds (listener)

litter 1. to leave rubbish lying about: *You should not drop litter in the street.*
2. a family of puppies born at the same time

little small in size or amount

live 1. to exist and be alive, not dead (life, lives): *Tom's grandfather lived until he was eighty.*
2. to dwell or reside in a place: *Jean lived in Wales when she was young.*

88 DICTIONARY

lizard a scaly reptile with four short legs and a long tail

llama a South American animal with long wool and two-toed feet

load to put a heavy weight or burden on or in somewhere

loaf 1. to be lazy and spend time idly (loafer): *William loafed around the house and did nothing all day.*
2. a shaped portion of dough cooked in an oven (loaves)

loathe to hate or dislike very much (loathing)

lobster a large, edible shell fish with huge pincers

local connected with or belonging to a particular place

loch a lake in Scotland

lock 1. to close with a key: *Joan locked the door behind her.*
2. a piece of hair: *The princess had golden locks which fell as ringlets.*
3. an enclosure in a canal with a gate at each end which allows ships to go from one level to another

locust a large winged insect like a grasshopper which does great damage to crops in hot countries

lodge to live in a place for a time (lodger, lodging)

lofty high

logic the science of reasoning and thought (logical)

lollipop a boiled sweet on the end of a stick

lonely alone and feeling sad about it

long 1. to have a great wish for (longing): *James longed to take part in the Olympic Games.*
2. drawn out in time or space: *The concert lasted a long time.*

longitude the distance east or west of a line that passes from the North Pole, through Greenwich to the South Pole

DICTIONARY 89

L

look 1. to turn one's eyes upon or observe: *When Kay looked at her watch it was midday.* 2. to appear or seem to be: *Ken looked very ill.*

loom 1. to emerge indistinctly: *The haunted house loomed out of the fog.* 2. a machine for weaving cloth from thread

loop to double a string or cord so as to fasten it around something

loosen to unfasten or make not so tight

loot to steal or plunder

lop-sided having one side larger or heavier than another

lorry a large vehicle or truck for carrying heavy loads

lose/lost to mislay and not be able to find (loss)

loud making a great sound or noise

lounge 1. to sit back in a lazy way: *The children lounged on the sofa to watch television.* 2. a sitting room with comfortable chairs

love to feel great affection for someone

low not high, shallow

lower 1. to make less high or let something down with a rope: *Jill lowered the bucket into the well.* 2. further down, below the others: *John was lower down the hill than the rest of the group.*

loyalty being faithful, true and trustworthy (loyal)

luck something that happens by chance, either good or bad (lucky)

luggage the bags and suitcases that a traveller puts clothes and belongings into when travelling

lukewarm not hot or cold, but halfway between

lull a pause or interval

lullaby a song to send a baby to sleep

lumber 1. to move heavily: *The lorry lumbered up the hill under the weight of its load.*
2. anything that takes up space and is useless: *There is a lot of lumber in our attic.*
3. timber cut and split ready for sale

luminous giving out a faint light in the dark

lump a small mass of matter of no particular shape, or a swelling

lunch a meal eaten in the middle of the day

lung the part of the body where air is breathed in and out to put oxygen in the blood

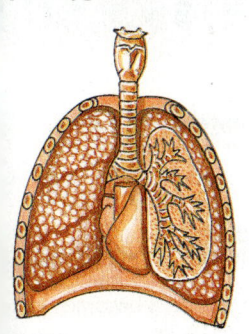

lurch to stagger or move suddenly and unexpectedly

lurk to lie hidden or in wait

luscious rich in taste and very good to eat

luxury great comfort, including costly possessions (luxurious)

M

machine an instrument or engine that does work by changing energy into movement (machinery)

magazine a paper that comes out regularly every month, quarter or year

maggot the small worm that develops from the eggs of a fly, often found in rotting food

magic pretending to do things that seem to be impossible (magician, magical)

magnet a piece of iron which attracts and draws other pieces of metal to it (magnetism, magnetic)

magnificent very splendid and grand

magnify to make something seem larger

mahogany a hard, reddish wood from a tropical tree

DICTIONARY 91

M

mail to send something through the post

maim to cripple or injure so that a limb cannot be used

main the principle or most important part

mainland the main part of a body of land, not an island

maize Indian corn, an important cereal crop

majesty the title of a sovereign; very grand and dignified

majority greater in number, quality or extent (major)

make to cause to be or do; to build or create (maker)

malaria a fever caused by a mosquito bite

male one of the sex that produces tiny cells that fertilize the eggs of a female (masculine)

malice ill–will, spite (malicious)

mammal an animal whose young are fed by the milk produced by the mother

manage to control; to succeed in doing something (manager, management)

mane the long hair on the neck of an animal such as a horse or lion

manger a trough in a stable for holding hay and food for cattle

manner a way of behaving or doing anything

mansion a large house with many rooms

mantelpiece a shelf over a fireplace

manufacture to make goods by hand or by machine

manure to put rotting organic waste into the ground so it becomes more fertile

manuscript a document written by hand

many a great number of

map a drawing to show the position of things such as towns, roads, etc.

92 DICTIONARY

M

marble a very hard, white stone used to make statues

March the third month of the year

march to walk with regular steps like soldiers

mare a female horse

margarine a fatty substance from plants that is used instead of butter

margin the border or edge

marigold a common garden flower with bright orange or yellow petals

marine found in, or connected with, the sea (mariner)

mark a visible sign such as a cross, dash or dot

market a public meeting place where goods are bought and sold

marmalade a jam made from oranges

maroon 1. to leave a person at a lonely spot: *After the shipwreck, the passengers were marooned on the island.*
2. a dark red colour

marquee a large tent

marrow 1. a fatty jelly found in the hollow centre of bones
2. a large oblong green-striped vegetable

marry to join two people together so they become husband and wife (marriage)

marsh very wet, low-lying ground

martyr a person who suffers great hardship or death for his beliefs

marvel to wonder at or be astonished (marvellous)

marzipan a sweet paste made from sugar and ground almonds

DICTIONARY 93

M

mascot a person or thing that will bring good luck

mask to put a cover over

mason a person who shapes stones for buildings

mass 1. a large amount or number (massive): *The garden is a mass of flowers.*
2. a religious celebration of the Catholic church

massacre to kill or murder a large number of people

massage to rub and knead the body to cure aches and pains

mast the tall pole on a boat or ship that supports the sails

master 1. to direct and control the actions of others: *The dog fetched the stick for its master.*
2. to manage and become good at doing something (mastery): *Fred soon mastered the art of water skiing.*

match 1. to be the same in size, shape or colour: *The colour of Flora's dress matched the blue of her eyes.*
2. a small stick tipped with a substance which lights when it is rubbed against a rough surface: *Bob lit the candles with a match.*
3. a sporting contest: *Jean was keen to play in the tennis match.*

mate 1. to make a pair: *Birds usually mate in the spring.*
2. a companion or helper: *Jock wanted to go to the football match with his mates.*
3. the second in command on a ship

material the stuff of which anything is made

mathematics the science that deals with numbers (mathematician)

matinee an afternoon performance at a theatre

matron 1. the head nurse in a hospital
2. the woman who looks after the housekeeping in a boarding school

94 DICTIONARY

matted a tangled mass

matter 1. to be of importance or trouble: *It does not matter to me what you do.* 2. a substance or material: *Leaves have a green colouring matter inside them.*

mattress a bag stuffed with feathers, straw or other matter, to make a soft bed on which to lie

mature to ripen (maturity)

mauve a light purple colour

maximum the greatest number or amount

May the fifth month of the year

may/might to show possibility or give permission

mayonnaise a thick sauce of egg yolk, oil and vinegar for salad

mayor the chief person of a town or city (mayoress)

maypole a tall pole decorated with flowers and ribbons that people dance around

maze a confusing arrangement of paths and turnings in which it is difficult to find one's way

meadow a level piece of grassland used for grazing cattle

meagre scarce, poor

meal food eaten at a certain time

mean/meant 1. to intend: *This present is meant for you.* 2. to make known or signify (meaning): *That sign does not mean you should drive faster.* 3. poor, shabby: *The streets were mean and dirty.* 4. stingy and selfish: *Bob was so mean he did not give his wife a birthday present.*

M

measles an infectious disease which causes a red rash on the skin

measure to find out the size or weight of something (measurement)

meat the flesh of an animal used as food

mechanic a person who works with machines (mechanical)

medal a piece of metal like a coin given as a prize or reward

meddle to interfere (meddler)

medicine drugs used to treat a disease (medical)

medium in the middle

meek humble, gentle

meet/met to come together (meeting)

megaphone a large speaking trumpet which makes the voice seem louder at a distance

melancholy sad and gloomy

mellow soft and ripe, well matured

melody a song or tune

melon a large juicy fruit with a centre full of seeds

melt to make or become liquid (molten)

member one of a society or group of people (membership)

memory the part of the mind that remembers things that have happened or been learned

menace to threaten

menagerie a collection of wild animals kept in cages and taken around the country for show

mend to improve or make better something that has been damaged

mental connected with the mind or brain

mention to speak about briefly

menu a list of different foods served at a meal

merchant a person who buys and sells goods from foreign countries

mercy kindness and forgiveness (merciful)

mere nothing more than (merely)

M

meringue a mixture of sugar and egg white whipped until stiff and baked until dry and crumbly

merit to earn or deserve

mermaid an imaginary sea creature with the upper body and head of a woman, and the tail of a fish

merry jolly and cheerful

mess a muddle or state of disorder

message information sent by one person to another (messenger)

metal substances such as gold, iron and copper that are found in the earth

meteor a sudden streak of light in the sky caused by a particle burning up as it passes through the Earth's atmosphere

meter a machine to measure the amount of water, gas or electricity used

method a way of doing something (methodical)

metre a measurement of length (metric)

mew the sound made by a cat

microlight a very small aircraft for one or two people

microphone an instrument for turning sound waves into electrical waves so they can be sent as radio signals

microscope an instrument that makes very tiny things appear larger

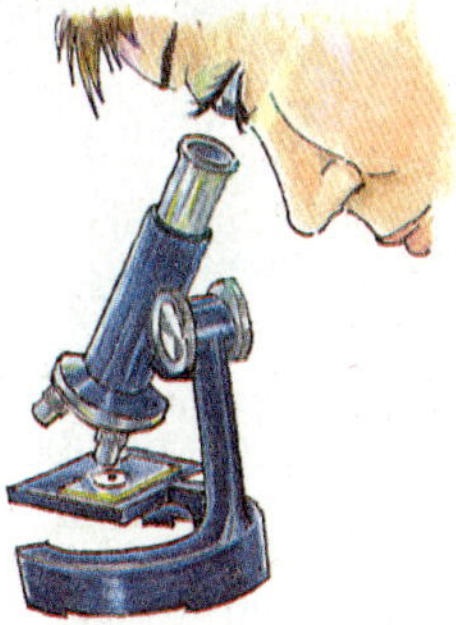

middle the point half way between two ends

DICTIONARY 97

M

midge a small winged insect which gives a nasty bite in the summer

midnight twelve o'clock at night

might power, strength

migrate to leave one country and go to live in another

mild gentle, kind, calm

mile a measurement of distance

military connected with soldiers

milk the white fluid produced by female mammals to feed their young

mill a building with machinery for grinding

million a thousand thousands (1,000,000)

mimic to imitate or copy someone in order to make fun of them (mime)

mince to chop into very small pieces

mincemeat a mixture of currants, raisins, spices and nuts used to make Christmas pies

mind 1. to look after or pay attention to: *Susan minded the baby while her parents went shopping.*
2. to object to or care about: *Pete did not mind where he went on holiday.*
3. the part of the brain where we think or learn

mine to dig coal and other substances from a deep hole in the ground (miner, mineral)

miniature very small

minnow a very small freshwater fish often used as bait

minor small, not serious or important

mint 1. to make coins
2. a herb used to flavour food and some sweets

minus to take away from or make less

minute (say <u>min</u>it) a measurement of time; sixty seconds

minute (say my<u>newt</u>) very small

98 DICTIONARY

M

miracle a wonderful happening (miraculous)

mirror a glass or polished surface that reflects light

mirth fun, happy laughter

miscellany a mixture of different things (miscellaneous)

mischief harm or damage, the cause of trouble (mischievous)

miser a person who is mean and stingy with money (miserly)

misery great unhappiness (miserable)

misfortune bad luck, a disaster

mislead to deceive, either on purpose or by mistake

misprint a mistake in printing

missile 1. something thrown to cause harm: *The angry crowd threw stones and other missiles at the police.* 2. a rocket–like weapon

mission a group of people sent to another country to discuss important matters, or to teach religion (missionary)

mist a cloud of very fine droplets or rain that is difficult to see through

mistake to make an error or be wrong about something

mistletoe a climbing plant with white berries used as a decoration at Christmas

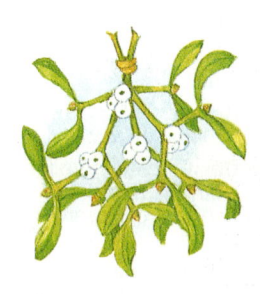

mite a very small insect

mix to put different things together (mixture)

moan to give a low cry of grief or pain

moat a deep ditch around a castle, usually filled with water

DICTIONARY 99

M

mobile easily moved

mock 1. to make fun of in an unkind way: *Nigel was mocked for his strange way of talking.* 2. imitation, not real: *The trifle was covered in mock cream.*

model to make a shape or an exact copy of something

moderate to become less violent; average

modern up-to-date in ideas; in the manner or fashion of the present day

modesty to be quiet and not conceited about something (modest)

moisten to make wet and damp (moisture)

mole 1. an animal that lives underground with velvety brown fur and very small eyes

2. a small brown spot on the skin

moment a short space of time (momentary)

monastery a building where monks live

Monday the second day of the week

money paper notes and coins used to buy things

monk a member of a religious community who spends his time in prayer and good works

monkey a hairy mammal with arms and legs which lives in trees and has paws like the hands of humans

monotony something dull and boring, with no change or variety (monotonous)

monsoon a wind bringing very heavy rainfall in South East Asia

monster a large creature of strange shape or appearance, often thought of as wicked and cruel (monstrous)

M

month one of the 12 parts into which a year is divided

monument a statue or pillar put up in memory of a person or an event (monumental)

mood a state of mind (moody)

moon the planet that travels around the Earth

moor 1. an open stretch of land covered with grass and low growing plants
2. to tie up a ship or boat in harbour (mooring)

moral 1. knowing the difference between right and wrong (morality)
2. a lesson learned from a story or from something that happens: *The moral of the story is that you should always be kind to other people.*

morning the time of day between dawn and midday

morse a system of dots and dashes used to send messages

morsel a small piece of food

mortar the cement between the bricks of a building

mosque a building where Muslims go to pray

mosquito a small flying insect that can cause a disease called malaria from its bite

moss a small green plant that grows in damp places

moth an insect like a butterfly, that flies at night

mother the female parent of a child

motion movement

motive reason or purpose

motor an engine that causes movement (motorist)

DICTIONARY 101

M

motorcycle a heavy, two-wheeled bicycle with an engine

motorway a road with two or more lanes of traffic in each direction, and few junctions

motto a short phrase or sentence that gives advice or teaches a lesson

mould 1. to form into a shape: *Peter moulded the plasticine to make a duck.*
2. a bluish coloured fungus which grows on food, damp leather, cheese or bread

moult to shed feathers, hair or skin which is then replaced by new growth

mound a heap of earth or sand

mount 1. to climb up on the back of an animal: *Roger mounted the horse and then set off on his ride.*
2. a mountain or hill
3. to put in a frame or special setting: *Paul mounted the photographs in an album.*

mountain a very high hill

mourn to feel great sorrow (mourner, mourning)

mouse a small, furry animal that lives in fields and under the floor of houses (mice)

moustache the hair that grows on a man's upper lip

mouth 1. the part of the face between the lips through which food is taken
2. an opening or entrance (mouth of a river)

move to change position or take from one place to another (movement)

mow to cut long grass (mower)

muddle untidiness or confusion

mulberry a dark sweet fruit like a blackberry that grows on a tree

multiply to make or become more in number (multiplication)

mumble to utter muffled sounds

M

mummy a dead body preserved from decay by the ancient Egyptians

munch to chew

murder to kill a person deliberately

murmur to speak in a soft, low voice

muscle a bundle of tissues in the body that contracts to produce movement (muscular)

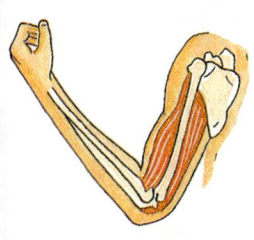

museum a building where works of art, objects of natural history etc. are kept for public display

mushroom an edible fungus shaped like a small umbrella

music sounds or notes combined to make a pattern that is pleasant to listen to (musician)

mussel a small, edible shellfish with two shells hinged together

mustard a yellow powder with a hot taste

musty with a stale taste or smell

mute silent

mutiny a refusal to obey orders (mutineer)

mutter to speak in a low voice (muttering)

mutton the flesh of a sheep used for eating

muzzle 1. a sort of cage put over the mouth of a dog or horse to stop it biting people

2. the open end of a gun

myriad a very large number, too many to count

mystery something strange that cannot be explained (mysterious)

mystify to puzzle or confuse

myth a story or legend of long ago that no one knows if true

DICTIONARY 103

N

nail 1. the flat hard covering at the end of fingers and toes 2. a metal pin with a flat head for fastening wood etc.

naked having no clothes on, bare

name the word by which any person or thing is known

nanny a children's nurse, or guardian

nape the back of the neck

napkin a square of cotton or linen cloth used to wipe the lips during a meal

narrate to tell a story (narrator, narrative)

narrow not wide or broad

nasty unpleasant

nation people living in a country under one government

native a person who is born in a country and still lives there

nature 1. the world of things not made by man eg. plants, animals, the sea, the sky (natural): *Bill liked nature study and all wild animals.* 2. the character or main qualities of a person or animal: *Jane had an open, friendly nature.*

naughtiness bad behaviour (naughty)

nausea a feeling of sickness (nauseous)

navigate to steer a boat or vessel (navigator, navigation)

navy the warships of a country and their crew

near close by

neat clean and tidy

necessary needed, cannot do without

nectar the sweet, sugary juice made by flowers

neck the part of the body that joins the head to the trunk

necklace a string of beads or precious stones worn around the neck

need to want or require (necessity)

needle a sharp pointed instrument with a hole at one end through which thread is passed when sewing

needy in need of help

104 DICTIONARY

N

negative 1. expressing refusal or denial: *When Bill asked if he could go with James to the cinema, James replied in the negative.* 2. photographic film in which the light and dark shades are reversed

neglect to treat without care and affection

neigh the sound made by a horse

neighbour the person who lives next door, or very near

neither not one or the other

nephew the son of a person's brother or sister

nerve one of the bundles of fibres in the body which pass messages to the brain from the skin, eyes, nose, etc.

nest the home built by a bird to rear the young birds

nettle a common weed with hairs which give a nasty sting

neutral not taking one side or the other in an argument or war

never not ever

new not known or existing before

news fresh information about recent events

newspaper a printed paper that gives the news

newt an animal with a long tail like a lizard that lives both in the water and on land

DICTIONARY 105

N

nibble to bite off small pieces at a time

nickname a name given to show friendship or make fun of someone

next the nearest, or immediately following, in place or time

nice pleasant, agreeable

niece the daughter of a person's brother or sister

night the time of darkness between sunset and sunrise

nightingale a small bird with a beautiful song

nightmare a very bad dream

nimble able to move quickly and easily

noble 1. a person of high birth or rank with a title eg. earl or baron 2. worthy of respect or admiration

nobody not anyone

nocturnal happening or active during the night

noise a loud or unpleasant sound

nomad a person who travels from place to place, with no fixed permanent home

nonsense having no sense or meaning

noon midday

normal ordinary, usual

north the region or point on the compass opposite to the midday sun

nose the bump on the face that juts out above the mouth and is used to breathe

nostril one of the two openings in the nose

note 1. to pay attention to: *Mark noted the time when the trains left.* 2. to write a short letter: *Kate's mother wrote a note to the school to say she was sick.*

notebook a small book for writing notes

nothing not anything

notice to see and pay attention to

nourish to give food to

novel 1. a book containing a long story: *Belinda preferred novels to short stories.* 2. new or unusual: *Hang gliding was a novel experience for Geoff.*

O

November the eleventh month of the year

now at this moment

nowhere not in any place

nudge to push lightly with the elbow in order to attract attention

nuisance something which is troublesome or annoying

numb without any feeling because of the cold

number a word used to show how many or how great the quantity is

numerous very many

nurse to look after a sick person or a child (nursery)

nutriment food that helps growth (nutrient, nutritious)

nylon a strong artificial thread which looks like silk

oak a slow-growing tree with hard wood that produces its seed as acorns

oar a long pole that is flat at one end and used to row a small boat

oasis a place in the desert where the underground water is near the surface so trees and plants can grow

oath a solemn promise

obey to do as one is told (obedience)

object (say objekt) to be against or in opposition to (objection): *Anne objected to the new motorway.*

DICTIONARY 107

O

object (say <u>ob</u>jekt) 1. a thing: *Jean saw a strange object in the sky.*
2. a purpose or reason: *The object of the game was to win as many points as possible.*

oblong a shape with square corners and two sides longer than their opposite two sides

observe to notice or to study carefully (observation)

obstacle something that is in the way

obstinate unwilling to change one's mind or give way to others

obstruct to block the way and prevent anything passing (obstruction)

obtain to get

obvious easily seen or understood

occasionally from time to time, not all the time

occupy 1. to be busy with something (occupation): *Watching birds occupied a lot of John's time.*
2. to live in a place or to take possession of: *Jenny's family occupied a house in the country.*

occur to happen (occurrence)

ocean the great body of water surrounding the land parts of the Earth

October the tenth month of the year

octopus a sea creature with eight arms covered with suckers for moving and catching food

odd unusual, strange

odour a smell (odorous)

offend 1. to do something wrong (offence): *The judge punished the thief for offending against the law.*
2. to hurt someone's feelings: *Joy was offended when Kate arrived late for the party.*

108 DICTIONARY

O

offer to present or give something

office a room in a building where business is done (official)

officer a person who has an important position, especially in the armed forces

offspring children of particular parents

often many times, frequently

oil a liquid obtained from the fossil remains of animals that lived millions of years ago, or from plants (oily)

oilskin a waterproof coat

ointment an oily paste used to cure skin troubles

old having lived a long time, not new or modern

omen a sign or warning that something is going to happen (ominous)

omit to leave out (omission)

once not repeated, at one time only

onion an edible bulb with fleshy leaves and a strong smell and taste

only the single or sole example

ooze to flow or leak out very slowly

opal a jewel with different colours sparkling in a background of milky white, pink or greenish blue

open to take away an obstruction and allow free movement or passage (opening)

opera a play set to music

operate 1. to make something work: *Chris operated the machinery to grind the corn.*
2. to cut out the diseased or repair the damaged part of a body (operation): *The surgeon operated on Ruth's leg to remove the lump.*

DICTIONARY 109

O

opinion an idea or belief

opportunity a chance to do something

oppose to be against or on the other side (opposition)

optical connected with the sight of the eye

oral connected with the mouth; spoken, not written

orator a person who gives speeches in public (oration)

orange 1. a colour made by mixing red and yellow
2. the round juicy golden-coloured fruit of a citrus tree

orchard a piece of land where fruit trees grow

orchestra a group of musicians who play together

order 1. to arrange in a tidy way: *Ben ordered the pencils by colour.*
2. to tell someone to do something: *The head teacher ordered everyone to stop talking.*

ordinary usual, not special

organ 1. a part of the inside of the body such as the lungs or stomach
2. a musical instrument with pipes and keys like a piano

organise to arrange or set in working order (organisation)

Orient The East (oriental)

origin the start or beginning of something (original)

ornament a thing used to decorate or adorn (ornamental)

orphan a child whose parents are dead

ostrich a large bird with a long neck and long legs which cannot fly

ought to be obliged to

outing a pleasure trip or excursion

outlast to last longer than

outlaw a person who does not obey the laws

outnumber to be more in number

outskirts the outer edges of a place or town

oval egg shaped

oven a metal box which is heated up to cook food in it

overalls a loose garment worn to protect the clothing underneath from dirt

overboard over the side of a ship

overcoat a warm coat worn on top of other clothing

overcrowded with too many people

overhead above the head

owe to have a duty to pay money to someone

owl a bird with keen hearing and silent flight that hunts for food at night

ox a strong animal like a bull (oxen)

oyster a shellfish that is eaten as a food

P

pace to walk or move

pack 1. to arrange in a bag, box or suitcase so as to take up as little space as possible (packing)
2. a group of animals or people (pack of wolves)
3. a bundle of goods carried on the back (back pack)

package a number of things wrapped up together

paddle 1. to walk in the sea with bare feet
2. to move a boat through water using a single, wide oar, or a pair.

paddock a field where horses are kept

P

padlock a lock with a hoop used to fasten doors and gates

pagan a person who worships idols or false gods

page 1. one side of a leaf of a book or piece of paper
2. a boy who helps in a hotel or helps look after royalty

pageant a show or procession with persons wearing historical costumes

pail a bucket

pain a feeling of soreness or aching (painful)

paint to spread colours over the surface (painter, painting)

pair two things of a kind

palace a building where royalty live (palatial)

palate the roof of the mouth

pale without much colour

palette a thin oval board used by artists to mix paint

palm 1. the broad, flat inner surface of the hand
2. a tree with a thin trunk and leaves at the top that produces dates

pamphlet a thin, paper-covered book

pancake a thin cake of batter made from flour, milk and eggs, fried in a pan

pang a sudden pain

panic a sudden fear or terror

pant to breathe quickly

panther a kind of leopard with a dark fur

pantomime a Christmas show based on a fairy tale

paper a material made from wood, straw or rags which is used for wrapping, writing on, and printing

parable a story with a double meaning which teaches a moral

112 DICTIONARY

P

parachute a large umbrella–shaped piece of cloth attached to ropes which slows down the fall to earth of a person or thing

parade to walk in a procession

paradise heaven

paraffin a kind of oil used for lighting or heating

paragraph a section or division of a piece of writing

parallel side by side and always the same distance apart

paralyse to prevent movement of the limbs (paralysis)

parcel a bundle or package

parched very dry or thirsty

parchment the skin of a sheep or goat used for writing on

pardon to forgive

parent the mother or father of a child

park a public garden with grass and trees

parrot a brightly coloured tropical bird with a large hooked beak

parsley a green herb with crinkly leaves

parsnip a root vegetable like a large carrot with a white flesh

part a portion or bit of something

particle a very small bit or portion

particular special, not general

partition to divide or separate off

partner a person who does something together with another

partridge a small game bird

DICTIONARY 113

P

party a number of people who do the same thing together

pass 1. to go by or through: *Bill passed the church on his way to school.*
2. to succeed in an examination
3. to move something from one person to another: *Dad asked Kim to pass the honey.*

passage 1. a narrow hall or corridor
2. a sea journey
3. a part of a book or speech

passenger a traveller on board a ship, plane or train

passport an official document which gives details about a person who wants to travel abroad

password a word one has to say to a guard in order to enter a place

past at an earlier time, not in the present

paste to stick with a glue or thick sticky mixture

pasteurise to kill any germs by heating

pastry a cake made of flour and fat used to cover pies

pasture grass fields where sheep and cattle graze

patch to mend a hole by covering it with a small piece of material or cloth

path a track where people can walk

patience calm and long suffering, not easily made angry (patient)

pattern 1. a shape that is to be copied: *Jean bought a knitting pattern to make a jumper.*
2. a design or markings on something: *Sue had a pattern of ducks on her sweater.*

pauper a very poor person

pause to stop for a short time

pave to make a level surface of stone or brick (pavement)

pavilion a small building on a sports ground

paw the foot of an animal

pay to give money in return for something (payment)

pea edible, round green seeds of the garden vegetable

peace quietness, calm, not at war

peach a juicy fruit with a velvety skin and a hard stone in the middle

peacock a large bird, the male of which has beautifully coloured tail feathers which it spreads out in a fan

peak 1. the top of a mountain

2. the part of a cap which shades the eyes

peal the sound of bells ringing

peanut a seed that grows in a pod underground that is used for its oil, or is dried and salted

pear a juicy fruit with a yellow skin and pips like an apple

pearl a precious stone that develops inside the shell of an oyster

peasant a country person who works on the land

peat a brown turf that is cut and dried and used as fuel instead of coal

pebble a small, round stone

peck to pick up with the beak

peculiar strange, unusual

pedal to turn a machine by using a lever operated by the foot

DICTIONARY 115

P

pedestrian a person who walks

peel to take the skin off

peep to take a quick look through a narrow opening

peer to look closely and carefully

pelican a water bird with webbed feet and a pouch under its large bill

pellet a small round ball of anything

penalty a punishment

pencil a stick with lead in the middle that is used for writing and drawing

penetrate to pierce or push through (penetration)

penguin a sea bird with webbed feet and flippers instead of wings, that lives in the Antarctic

peninsula a piece of land that juts out into the sea and is almost surrounded by it

penknife a small knife which folds up and can be carried in the pocket

people any group of persons; a race or nation

pepper a hot powdery spice to season food

perch 1. to sit on the edge
2. a freshwater fish

perennial lasting for several years

perfect complete, without any faults

perform to take part in a play, concert or ceremony (performer, performance)

perfume a sweet scent or smell

peril danger

period a portion of time

P

periscope an instrument with a series of mirrors which allows someone at a lower level to see surrounding objects above the crowd or surface

perish to die, decay or be destroyed

permanent remaining the same for a long time

permit to allow (permission)

perpetual never ending, lasting for ever

persevere to keep on trying (perseverance)

persist to keep on doing something in spite of difficulties (persistence)

person a human being (personal)

perspire to sweat (perspiration)

persuade to win over and make someone do something they were previously unwilling to do (persuasion)

pest a troublesome or harmful thing or person

pester to trouble or annoy

petal a coloured leaf in a flower

petition to ask someone to do something

petrol the fuel burned in a motor vehicle

petroleum an oil obtained from fossil fuel

petticoat an underskirt

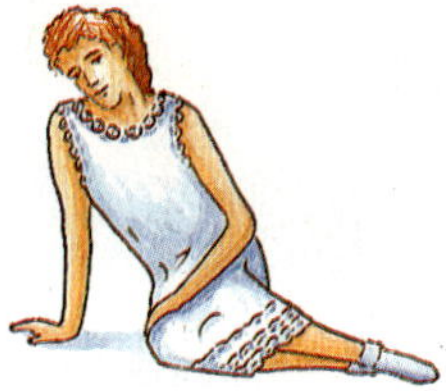

petty small and unimportant

pew a long wooden seat in a church

pewter a dull grey metal made from tin, lead or other metal

phantom a spirit or ghost

pheasant a game bird with a long tail and brilliant feathers

phone to speak to someone on a telephone

photograph to take a picture of someone by using the action of light on a light–sensitive film (photographer, photography)

phrase a small group of words forming part of a sentence

DICTIONARY 117

P

physical connected with the body and the senses

piano an instrument with black and white keys to play music

pick 1. to choose or select: *Kay picked out the ripest cherries from the basket.*
2. to take up with finger and thumb: *Roger picked a bunch of flowers for his mother.*
3. an instrument for digging with a pointed metal head: *The earth was so hard that Jim had to break it up with a pick.*

pickle to preserve in vinegar and spices

pickpocket a person who steals from the pocket of another

picnic an informal meal outdoors

picture a drawing or painting of something

pie a dish of meat or fruit covered with pastry

piece a separate part or bit of anything

pier a long platform built out over water from the shore

pierce to make a hole in

pigeon a bird with grey feathers belonging to the dove family

pile to put in a heap

pilfer to steal small amounts

pilgrim a person who travels to a holy place (pilgrimage)

pill a small ball of medicine that is swallowed whole

pillar an upright column to support part of a building

pillow a soft cushion to rest the head on at night

pilot to steer a plane or a ship

pincers a metal tool for gripping things

pinch to nip or squeeze between thumb and forefinger

P

pine 1. to long for or grow thin and ill from grief: *The puppy pined for its mother and would not eat.*
2. an evergreen tree that bears its seeds in cones

pineapple a large juicy yellow fruit with a prickly golden skin and prickly green leaves on top

pink a pale red colour made by mixing red and white paint

pioneer an explorer who prepares the way for others

pipe a long tube or funnel

pirate a sailor who robs other ships on the high seas

pistol a small hand gun

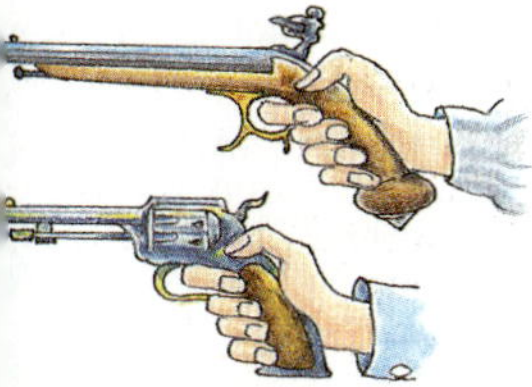

pitch 1. to throw or toss something: *Derek pitched the ball into the long grass.*
2. a thick black substance like tar used in making roads
3. to set up a stall in the market: *Jane pitched her stall near the post office.*
4. the place where a game is played (football pitch)

pity to feel sympathy or feel sorry for someone

pizza a flat dough base topped with a savoury mixture of tomatoes and cheese

place to put in a particular spot

placid calm, peaceful

plague 1. to annoy or trouble: *The midges plagued us every evening on holiday.*
2. deadly disease that spreads rapidly: *Many people died of the plague.*

plaice a flat fish used as food

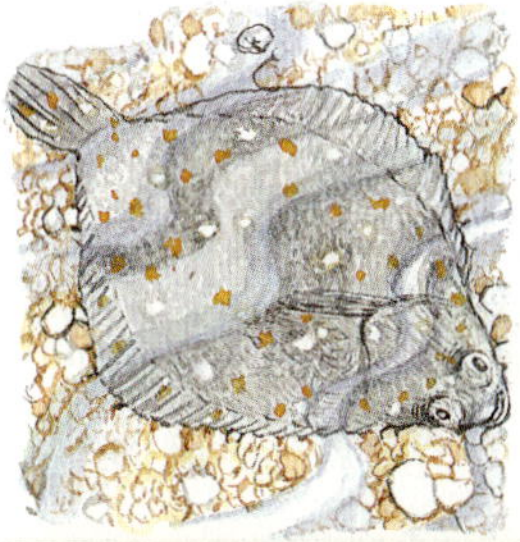

DICTIONARY 119

P

plain 1. simple, without any decoration: *Dave wore a plain white shirt, but Tom's was brightly coloured.*
2. a flat, level space: *The giraffes grazed among the trees on the plain.*

plait to twist two or more strands or strips into a long rope

plan 1. to arrange something beforehand: *Fred and Mary planned to take a holiday in Greece.*
2. a drawing or diagram: *Kate made a plan of her house.*

plane 1. to make wood smooth with a carpenter's tool: *The carpenter planed down the rough edges of the bench.*

2. a tree with broad leaves

3. flat open land
4. a short form of aeroplane

planet a ball of rock that circles a sun

plank a long flat piece of wood

plant to put seeds or vegetables, flowers, bushes etc. in the ground so they will grow

plaster 1. to cover with a thick coating of lime, sand and water: *Derek plastered the walls of his house.*
2. a strip of material put over a wound to keep the germs out

plastic a material made from oil that is moulded into different shapes

plate a shallow, round dish from which food is eaten

plateau a level stretch of ground high above sea level

platform a wooden structure raised above the level of the floor or ground

play 1. to take part in a game or amuse oneself (player): *The children played hide and seek together.*
2. a show acted in a theatre: *Gill went to see the play about robots last week.*

plead to beg or ask earnestly (plea)

pleasant nice, enjoyable

please to give enjoyment or happiness (pleasure)

plenty enough or more than enough (plentiful)

pliers small pincers with a tight grip

plot 1. to make a secret plan: *Guy Fawkes plotted to blow up Parliament.*
2. a small piece of ground: *Peter grew vegetables on his plot of land.*
3. the story of a play, book or film: *The plot of the murder film was very complicated.*

plough to turn up the earth with a machine

pluck 1. courage (plucky): *Jean plucked up courage to climb the ladder.*
2. to pull the feathers out: *Dick plucked the turkey at Christmas.*

plum a round or oval fruit with a juicy flesh and a hard stone

plumber a person who looks after the water and sewage works in a building

plume a large, soft feather

plump rather fat

plunder to take by force

plunge to throw oneself headlong into

pneumatic containing air

pneumonia an illness caused by inflammation of the lungs

DICTIONARY 121

P

poach 1. to take game or fish from someone's property without permission (poacher) 2. to cook an egg in water without its shell

pocket a small bag sewn into clothes for carrying things such as keys or a handkerchief

poem a pattern of words that is also usually a pattern of sounds as well (poet, poetry)

point 1. to show by indicating with a forefinger: *Julie pointed to the toy she wanted her mother to buy.* 2. the sharp end of something: *Bill sharpened the points of his pencils.* 3. the exact place: *The tourists gathered at their point of departure.*

poison to give someone a substance which can harm or kill

pole 1. a long, rounded piece of wood or metal 2. the furthest north or the furthest south part of the world (polar)

police people who help keep law and order

polish to rub until shiny

polite well-bred and well spoken

pond a large pool of water

pony a small horse

poodle a dog with thick, curly hair often clipped into tufts

pool a small amount of water or other liquid

poplar a tall, thin tree with shiny, trembling leaves

popular pleasing to many people

population the number of people living in a place

porch a covered entrance to a doorway

pore 1. a tiny hole in the skin (porous) 2. to look at closely: *John pored over the drawings in the book.*

122 DICTIONARY

pork the flesh of a pig when used as food

porridge a breakfast dish made from oatmeal and water

port 1. a harbour
2. a sweet red wine
3. the left side of a ship, looking forwards

portable able to be easily carried

portcullis a strong grating across the entrance to many castles that is lowered to keep out enemies

porter a person who carries bags and parcels

port-hole a small round window in the side of a ship

portion a part or share of something

portrait a painting or photograph of someone

position 1. the way something or someone is placed: *Sarah was crouched down in a very uncomfortable position.*
2. a place: *Jack tried to find the ship's position on the chart.*
3. employment: *Jane tried to find a position as a teacher.*

positive certain, sure

possess to own or have (possession)

possible likely to happen

post 1. an upright piece of wood or metal
2. the carrying and delivering of letters and parcels
3. a position or job: *Ann held the post of hotel manager.*

postcard a card with a picture on one side and space for a message on the other which is sent through the post

poster a large picture or advertisement put up in a public place

DICTIONARY 123

P

postpone to put off to a later date (postponement)

potato a garden vegetable which stores food in underground roots that are round and can be eaten

potent powerful

potion a drink of medicine or poison

pottery dishes or ornaments made from clay and baked hard in a kiln (potter)

pouch a bag or pocket

poultry birds such as chickens, ducks and geese

pounce to seize or jump on suddenly

pound to crush into powder

pour to come out in a stream

poverty having little or no money (poor)

powder dust

power 1. strength or ability to do things (powerful): *Ken had the power to lift the heavy stone.*
2. control over or influence: *The King had power over all his subjects.*

practical useful, sensible

practise to do a thing regularly so as to get better at it (practice)

prairie a wide area of open grassland with no trees

praise to speak well of

pram a baby carriage

prawn a shell fish like a shrimp but larger

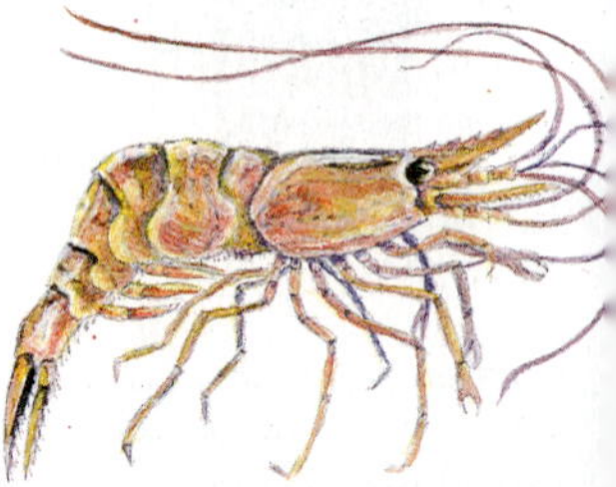

pray to ask God for something (prayer)

preach to give a talk about religion in public (preacher)

precaution something done to prevent trouble or danger

precious of great value or price

124 DICTIONARY

precipice a steep cliff

precise exact (precision)

predict to say or tell beforehand what will happen (prediction)

prefer to like one thing better than another (preference)

prehistoric belonging to the time before history was written down

prejudice to form a hasty opinion without a fair examination of the facts

prepare to make a thing ready (preparation)

present 1. to give something: *Julia presented her mother with a bunch of flowers.* 2. to be at a certain place (presence): *Jill's parents were present at the school concert.*

preserve to keep safely, or to keep food from going bad

preside to be in charge of a meeting (president)

press 1. to push or squeeze (pressure): *Roger pressed the doorbell.*
2. to make smooth: *Karen pressed the trousers she wanted to wear.*
3. newspapers: *Billy read about the accident in the press.*

presume to suppose to be true without proof (presumption)

pretend to play at being a different person (pretence)

pretty attractive and pleasing to look at

prevent to stop or make something impossible to do (prevention)

previous happening before

prey to hunt and kill animals for food

price the sum of money that must be paid to buy something

DICTIONARY 125

P

prick to pierce slightly with a sharp point

pride a feeling of great satisfaction and self esteem (proud)

priest a minister of religion

prim behaving very correctly and formally

primrose a pale yellow spring flower

prince the son of a king or queen

princess the daughter of a king or queen

principal the most important person or leader

principle honesty; a moral or settled reason for action

print to press inked type on pages so as to reproduce words, pictures etc. (printer)

prison a building where criminals are kept (prisoner)

private belonging to or concerning only one person

privilege a special favour or advantage for only a few

prize a reward given for merit or success in a competition

probable likely to happen

problem a question that is difficult to answer or make up one's mind about

procession a number of people walking together in a special order

produce (say pro<u>dewce</u>) to bring forth or make; to show so it can be seen (produce, say pro<u>dewce</u>; production)

profession a job which needs special training (professional)

profit to gain advantage or extra money

programme a list of events

progress (say <u>progress</u>) to move forward (progress, say pro<u>gress</u>)

126 DICTIONARY

P

prohibit to forbid (prohibition)

promise to agree to do something

promote to move up to a higher position (promotion)

prompt 1. to help out an actor by reading the next words aloud 2. quick and ready to act

prong the sharp point of a fork or rake

pronounce to speak with the correct sound and accent (pronunciation)

prop to support and prevent from falling

propel to move something forward by force (propeller)

proper right and correct

property possessions and things that belong to you

prophesy to foretell or predict (prophecy)

propose to make a suggestion (proposal)

prosper to get on well or succeed (prosperity)

protect to guard or keep safe (protector, protection)

protest (say pro_test_) to object or complain about something (protest, say _pro_test)

prove to show something is right or correct (proof)

proverb a short saying which states a simple truth

provide to supply or prepare for (provisions)

provoke to anger or annoy (provocation)

prow the most forward part of a ship

prowl to roam about in search of prey

pry to be inquisitive and nosy

psalm a sacred song

public open for general use, not private or secret

publish 1. to make something generally known: _The vicar published the banns of marriage._
2. to make books and papers ready for printing and selling (publication)

pudding a sweet dish eaten after the main course

DICTIONARY 127

P

puddle a pool of muddy water

pull to draw towards one; to drag or tow

pullover a jersey or sweater put on by pulling it over the head

pulpit the raised wooden box in a church where the preacher stands

pulse the beating or throbbing of the heart which can be felt in the wrist

pump to raise up water with a machine

pumpkin a large, round, golden yellow fleshy garden vegetable

punch to strike with the clenched fist

punctual at the right time, not late

puncture a small hole in something that lets the air inside escape

punish to make someone suffer for their wrong-doing (punishment)

punt a small flat-bottomed boat

pupil a child being taught by a teacher

puppet a small doll with jointed limbs that moves by strings worked from above (puppeteer)

puppy a young dog

purchase to buy something

pure clean, fresh, unspoiled

purple a colour made by mixing blue and red

purpose the reason or intention

purr the noise made by a cat

purse a small bag or pocket to keep money

pursue to chase after (pursuit)

push to move or try to move away by pressing against something

pussy a cat

128 DICTIONARY

puzzle 1. a problem that is only solved after hard thinking 2. a toy with bits that lock together to form a picture

pygmy a very small person

pyjamas jacket and trousers worn in bed at night

pylon a metal tower or pillar to carry electricity cables

pyramid a building on a square base with triangular sides that rises to a single point, built by the ancient Egyptians to honour the dead

python a large non-poisonous snake that kills its prey by crushing and squeezing it

quack the sound made by a duck

quadruped a four-legged animal

quail a small game bird

quaint odd, usual and old-fashioned

quake to shake with fear

quality the nature of something, whether good or bad

qualm doubt or fear

quantity the amount or number

quarrel to disagree angrily with another

quarry a place where stone or rock is dug out

quarter half of a half; one of four equal parts

DICTIONARY 129

Q

quay a landing place, usually built of stone, where ships can tie up

queen 1. the wife of a king
2. a female head of a sovereign state

queer strange, unusual

query to ask about, to question

question to ask and try to find an answer

queue to form a line one behind the other

quick rapid, hasty

quicksand soft wet sand in which a person or animal might sink

quiet not noisy, calm

quill a large feather from a bird's wing

quilt a bedcover made from a bag filled with soft feathers then stitched across to form a pattern

quite entirely; rather

quiver 1. to tremble
2. a case for holding arrows

quiz a game where each side wins points for answering questions

quote to repeat words written or spoken by another

R

rabbit a small animal with a fluffy white tail that lives in a burrow underground

race to run swiftly in a competition

rack a wire shelf with spaces between the wires

racquet a stringed bat used to play tennis

radar a machine that uses the reflection of radio waves to tell the position of an object too far away to see, in the dark or in fog

radiate to send out rays eg. of heat (radiator, radiation)

radio a machine that receives signals sent out by a transmitter and turns them into sounds

radius the line from the centre of a circle to the circumference

R

raft logs or planks tied together so as to float

rafter a beam of wood that helps hold up the roof of a house

rage to be very angry

raid to make a sudden attack

rail a metal or wooden bar which is fixed to a post at either end (railing)

railway a track made of metal bars for trains to run on

rain drops of water that fall from the sky

rainbow an arch of coloured light that sometimes appears in the sky after a rainfall

raise to lift up (rise)

raisin a dried grape used in cakes and puddings

rake to scrape together using a long handled instrument with prongs at the end

rally to collect or gather round

ram 1. to push hard and violently against something: *Roger rammed the door back into its frame.*
2. a male sheep

ramble to walk for pleasure (rambler)

ranch a large sheep or cattle farm (rancher)

random by chance, without any pattern

range 1. to place in order or in line: *Jean ranged the carrots by size.*
2. to roam or wander (ranger): *The sheep ranged all over the hills.*
3. a row of mountains

rank 1. a row of things (taxi rank)
2. a position of importance: *Sam's dad held the rank of captain.*
3. having a bad, sour smell: *The weeds grew close and smelled rank.*

DICTIONARY 131

R

rapid fast, quick

rapids part of a river where the water rushes over a barrier of rocks

rare uncommon, few in number

rascal a bad or dishonest man

rash 1. foolish, unwise, too hasty: *Joy was rash to jump into the deep end of the pool.*
2. red spots on the skin

raspberry a sweet red fruit, like a blackberry without a centre

rate 1. a speed: *The rate the car was going was over 100 kilometres an hour.*
2. a value or price: *The rate for the job was very low.*

ration to allow a fixed amount of food or water for each person

rational sensible, reasonable

rattlesnake a poisonous snake that makes a rattling sound with its tail

ravenous very hungry

raw not cooked

ray a narrow beam of light

razor a tool for shaving a man's beard or moustache

reach 1. to arrive at, come to: *We were tired when we reached home after our walk.*
2. to stretch out a hand: *Billy reached out to stroke the baby elephant.*

read to look at and understand something that is written or printed (reader)

ready prepared, willing

real actually existing, not false or imaginary (reality)

realise to understand the truth of (realisation)

reap to cut ripe grain, to harvest (reaper)

rear 1. to bring up or grow: *Fred reared horses on his farm.*
2. to rise up on the hind legs: *The pony reared up in fright.*

3. the back part: *Jane sat in the rear seat of the car.*

reason 1. to argue with; to use the power of thinking or understanding: *Maria reasoned with her daughter and tried to get her to be more sensible.*
2. the cause or explanation: *The reason we were late for school was that we missed the bus.*

rebel (say re<u>bel</u>) to disobey orders (rebel, say <u>reb</u>el; rebellion)

recall 1. to remember: *Bob recalled when he was in Greece on holiday.*
2. to call back: *The teacher recalled Tom when he was about to go home.*

receipt 1. the act of receiving: *On receipt of Kay's letter, her mother immediately phoned her.*
2. a written notice that money or goods have been received: *The garage gave Jack a receipt for his car.*

receive to take or get from another, to accept (receiver, reception)

recent happening only a short time ago

recipe directions for preparing a dish of food

recite to repeat aloud (recitation)

reckless careless of danger

recognise to know again, identify (recognition)

recommend to speak well of a person to another (recommendation)

DICTIONARY 133

R

record (say re<u>kord</u>) to make a note of, in writing, or on a tape or disk (record, say <u>re</u>kord)

recorder 1. an instrument that makes or plays copies of sounds (cassette recorder)
2. a kind of flute

recover 1. to get back something (recovery): *John recovered the book he had dropped in the pond.*
2. to get better after an illness: *Jenny recovered from her cold within a week.*

re–cover to put a new cover on

rectangle a four–sided figure of which the angles are all right angles and the opposite sides are equal

recycle to make new products from materials that have been used already

redcurrant a shrub that bears clusters of small, red soft berries

reduce to make less or smaller in size (reduction)

reef 1. a line of rocks near the surface of the sea

2. to make a sail smaller by tying up or rolling up the lower portion

reel 1. to wind in a line or cord: *Peter reeled in his fishing line.*
2. a Scottish dance
3. to stagger about or sway from side to side: *Arthur reeled from the blow to his head.*

refer to send or go to for information (referee, reference)

refine to purify and take out unwanted matter (refinery)

134 DICTIONARY

reflect 1. to throw back light from a polished surface (reflection): *The mirror reflected the light from the window.* 2. to think about: *Roy reflected that he had not had a holiday for years.*

reform to make or become better (reformation)

refresh to make fresh or renew (refreshment)

refrigerate to make cold or frozen (refrigerator)

refuge a place of shelter or safety (refugee)

refund to pay back money

refuse (say re__fuse__) to say no to something (refusal)

refuse (say __re__fuse) rubbish, waste material

regain to get back something that has been lost

regard 1. to look at or consider: *Bill regarded the dog with suspicion.* 2. affection or care: *Amy had great regard for her aunt.*

region an area or place

regret to be sorry about

regular 1. happening at arranged or expected times (regularity): *There's a regular train service between London and Glasgow.* 2. obeying a rule; doing things by habit: *Jim made regular visits to the dentist.*

reign to rule over

rein the strap of a bridle used to control a horse

reindeer a kind of deer with branching horns found in northern lands

reject to refuse to accept; to throw away (rejection)

rejoice to be happy and glad (rejoicing)

relate to tell a story

relation a member of your family

relax to take things more easily (relaxation)

release to set free

relent to be less severe

DICTIONARY 135

R

relieve to free from care or pain (relief)

religion belief or faith in a god (religious)

reluctance unwillingness, dislike (reluctant)

rely to depend on or trust (reliance)

remain to stay behind (remainder)

remark to say or notice

remedy a cure

remember to keep in mind and not forget (remembrance)

remind to make someone remember (reminder)

remote far off and difficult to get to

remove to take or move away (removal)

renew to make as new again or restore

rent 1. a tear in a piece of cloth: *Tom's jacket had a large rent where he caught it on a branch.*
2. money paid regularly to live somewhere or to use something: *Anna rented a television set for a month.*

repair to mend

repeat to say or do again (repetition)

repel to drive back

repent to be sorry for doing wrong (repentance)

replace to put back; to get something in place of (replacement)

reply to answer

report 1. to bring or send news (reporter): *Ian reported that his sister was ill.*
2. to make or give a description of: *Cathy reported on the state of her garden.*

represent to act for or take the place of someone (representative)

reproduce 1. to make a copy (reproduction): *Jim reproduced the map of the village.*
2. to give new birth: *Mice reproduce up to five times a year.*

reptile a cold blooded animal with a tough, dry scaly skin

136 DICTIONARY

request to ask for

require to need (requirement)

rescue to save from danger

resemble to look like (resemblance)

resent to be angry or offended (resentment)

reserve 1. to keep or hold back (reservation): *Mike reserved some theatre seats.*
2. to be cautious and not show feeling: *Julie was reserved when she met her sister's friends.*

reservoir a store of water

resign to give up a position or work (resignation)

resist to be against or use force against (resistance)

resolve to decide or make up your mind (resolution)

resort a place where people go on holiday

respect to look up to, pay attention to

respond to reply (response)

responsible in charge of, trustworthy

rest 1. to stop moving and remain still and quiet, to sleep: *The children rested after their long walk.*
2. what is left over or remains: *The dog ate the rest of the food after the picnic.*

restaurant a building where people can buy meals

restless unable to keep still

restore to put back or make like new again (restoration)

DICTIONARY 137

R

result the end or consequence

retain to keep (retainer)

retire 1. to stop working at a certain age (retirement): *Bill retired when he was 65.* 2. to go away, depart: *Jane's parents retired to bed at eleven in the evening.*

retort to make a smart reply

retreat to go back

retrieve to get back, recover possession of (retrieval)

return 1. to go back: *The race horses returned to the starting line.* 2. to give or send back: *Robert returned the pen he had borrowed.*

reveal to show or make known (revelation)

revenge to return an injury for an injury in a spiteful way

reverse 1. to turn upside down or the other way around: *Jill reversed the position of the ornaments on the shelf.* 2. to change direction or go backwards: *Bob reversed the car into the garage.*

revise to look over and correct (revision)

revive to come back to life, to renew (revival)

revolt to rebel and rise up against

revolve to move or turn around a centre (revolution)

revolver a kind of pistol

reward to give in return for doing something well

rhinoceros a large, thick-skinned animal with one or two horns on its nose

rhyme to make words at the end of lines of verse sound like each other

rhythm a regular musical beat or succession of notes

ribbon a narrow strip of cloth or silk

rice a grain grown in Asia, one of the most important foods of the world

rich having plenty of money or goods

riddle a question made to puzzle the hearer

ride/rode to sit on and control a horse or bicycle, etc. (rider)

ridge 1. a long narrow hill
2. a raised strip of upturned soil in a ploughed field

ridicule to make fun of or mock

rifle 1. to search and rob: *The thief rifled through the house looking for money.*
2. a gun about a metre long

right 1. correct: *Ian gave the right answer to the question.*
2. the opposite of left

rigid stiff and not easily bent

ring/rang 1. to make a bell sound
2. a circle of something (circus ring)
3. to draw a circle around

rinse to wash out by filling with water; to remove soap suds in fresh water

riot to make a noise and disturb the peace

ripen to become fully developed and mature

rise/rose to stand or get up, to go upwards

risk to put in danger

rival to compete with another for success or reward (rivalry)

river a natural stream of water flowing in a channel towards the sea

road a prepared track or way for cars and other vehicles

roar to cry out with a full loud sound

DICTIONARY 139

R

roast to cook in an oven or over heat

robe a long outer garment or dress

robin a small bird, the male of which has a red breast

robot an automatic machine which works under the control of a computer

rock 1. a large mass of stone in the ground 2. to sway to and fro

rocket a cylinder-shaped tube which burns fuel to make it move forwards or upwards very quickly

rodent an animal with long front teeth for gnawing

rogue a rascal, a dishonest person

roll 1. to turn over and over: *The baby rolled the ball along the ground.*
2. bread or other food rolled to make a round tube

roller-skate a shoe with small wheels underneath

roof the top covering of a house

room a space in a house enclosed by walls

roost to rest or sleep as birds do on a perch

root the part of the plant below ground that anchors the plant in the soil

rope a strong line or cord made of twisted strands of fibre

rose a garden flower with bright petals and a sweet smell

rotate to turn around (rotation)

rough not smooth, uneven

round circular in shape, like a globe or sphere

roundabout a circle in the centre of a road junction that the traffic must go around

140 DICTIONARY

R

route the way to get somewhere

row (say <u>roe</u>) 1. to move a boat forwards with oars 2. a series of things in a straight line

row (say <u>rau</u>) a quarrel or noisy disturbance

royalty members of a king or queen's family (royal)

rubber the sticky sap of a tree which makes an elastic, bouncy material

rubbish waste matter

ruby a deep red precious stone

rudder the part at the back of a boat or plane used for steering

rude impolite

ruin to spoil or destroy

rule 1. to govern or control (ruler): *Queen Victoria ruled the country for many years.* 2. a law or order: *The teacher made it a rule that the children should not eat in class.*

rumour a story that has not been proved to be true

rung a step on a ladder

runway a straight, smooth path made for aircraft to take off and land on

rural connected with the country

rush 1. to move forward rapidly: *The policeman rushed to the scene of the accident.* 2. a plant with strong leaves found in wet, marshy places

rust to get covered with a reddish brown coating when iron or steel are left lying in damp places

S

sack 1. a large bag of coarse material 2. to steal and plunder a town after a battle

sacred holy; connected with the worship of a god

sacrifice to offer to a god; to give up or sell at a loss

saddle to put a leather seat on a horse

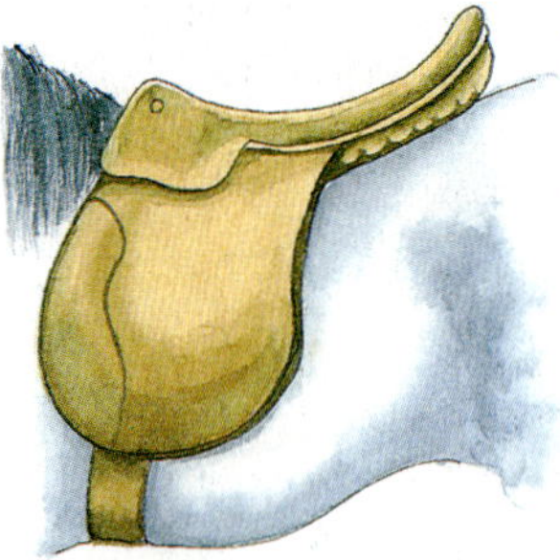

safety freedom from danger (safe)

sail 1. to set out on a voyage by ship (sailor): *The ship sailed to America once a week.* 2. a sheet of canvas stretched to catch the wind to make a ship move through the water: *Jenny hoisted the sails of the boat.*

saint a holy person

sake a reason or cause

salad a mixture of lettuce, tomatoes and other raw vegetables

salmon a large fish with orange-pink flesh

saloon a large public room in a hotel or ship

salt a substance used to season food

salute to greet (salutation)

same not different; identical or alike

sample 1. to test or try out: *Peter sampled the wine to find the best one.* 2. a small part of something that shows what the whole is like: *June took a sample of material to match the colours.*

sand fine, loose grains formed from broken rocks

sandal a light, open shoe

sandwich two slices of bread with a filling in between

sapphire a dark blue precious stone

142 DICTIONARY

S

sarcasm a bitter, cutting remark meant to hurt the listener (sarcastic)

sardine a small silver fish that lives in shoals

satin a smooth, shiny material

satisfy to make happy or contented (satisfaction)

Saturday the seventh day of the week

sauce a liquid that adds to the taste of meat, fish or puddings

saucepan a metal pot used for cooking

saucer a small, round shallow curved plate put under a cup to catch spilt liquid

sausage minced meat and seasoning or herbs stuffed into a thin skin

save to rescue from danger (safety)

savoury having a good taste; salty or spicy

saw a thin metal tool with teeth for cutting wood

scald to burn with a boiling liquid

scale 1. a machine to weigh or measure things
2. a number of musical notes which follow each other
3. to climb a steep cliff or mountain
4. the marks on a map which show the distances from place to place
5. the horny skin of some animals and fish

scalp the skin and hair covering the head

scamper to run about

scandal unkind gossip

scar a mark left on the skin by a cut or burn

scarcity in short supply (scarce)

scare to frighten

scarecrow a figure set up to frighten birds away from growing crops

scarf a cloth worn around the neck

DICTIONARY 143

S

scarlet bright red

scatter to throw about or move apart

scavenge to feed on dead animals or take away rubbish (scavenger)

scene 1. the place where a thing took place: *Hazel returned to the scene of the accident.* 2. a division of a play in the theatre (scenery) 3. a display of temper: *Roger made a scene when the train was late.*

scent 1. a pleasant smell 2. to track or follow by the smell of something

scheme to make a plan or plot

school a building where children are taught

science the study of natural phenomena (scientist)

scissors a tool with two sharp edges for cutting materials

scold to find fault with or tell off for wrong doing (scolding)

scooter a two-wheeled motor vehicle

scorch to burn slightly on the surface

score to win a point for runs or goals in a game or competition

scorn to dislike or look down on

scoundrel a bad person or rascal

scour to clean by rubbing

scowl to frown and look annoyed

scramble to climb on hands and feet

scrap 1. to throw out: *Bill scrapped his old bike because the wheel was bent.* 2. a small piece: *Jenny took a scrap of material to match the colours.*

scrape to clean with a knife or sharp tool

scratch to make a mark in a surface with a sharp point

scream to cry out in pain or fright

screech to make a harsh, shrill cry

screen to block off the light or wind

screw to fasten with a nail that has a spiral ridge around it to prevent it from being pulled out

screwdriver a tool to push in screws

scribble to write carelessly or draw meaningless lines

144 DICTIONARY

S

scrub to rub hard with a brush

sculptor a person who carves statues from stone or wood

scum a dirty froth on the surface of water

scurry to hurry or run with short quick steps

scythe to cut or mow with a sharp curved blade

sea the mass of salt water covering the greater part of the Earth

seagull a bird with grey feathers which lives by the sea

seal 1. to close up tightly so no air can get in: *William sealed the jar with wax.*
2. a sea animal with flippers to help it swim

seam the line where two edges join together

seaplane a plane with floats instead of wheels so that it can land and take off from water

search to look for something

seasick an illness brought on by the movement of a boat in the water

season 1. one of the four divisions of the year: *Winter is the coldest season.*
2. to make more tasty: *Joanna added salt and pepper to season the food.*

DICTIONARY 145

S

seat a thing made or used to sit upon

seaweed plants with leathery leaves and stems that grow in or beside the sea

second 1. very small division of time 2. the one after the first

secret something which is hidden and known to only a few people

secretary an office worker that helps write letters, keep records and prepare the business

security safety, freedom from fear or anxiety (secure)

seed the tiny fertilized egg from a female plant from which a new plant will grow

seek to look for

seem to appear to be

seesaw playground equipment where two children sit on either end of a long plank supported in the middle and move up and down alternately

seesaw

seize to snatch or grab; to take hold or possession of (seizure)

seldom not often

select to choose (selection)

selfish thinking more of oneself than of others

sell/sold to give in return for a sum of money (sale)

senior older, or of a higher rank or importance

send/sent to make something or a person go away

sense to feel or understand (sensation)

sentence 1. a group of words which convey a complete idea or thought: *A sentence begins with a capital letter and ends with a full stop.*
2. the punishment a judge orders for a prisoner: *The judge sentenced the criminal to five years' imprisonment.*

146 DICTIONARY

sentry a person who is on guard and gives a warning if anyone else comes near

separate (say separ<u>ate</u>) to divide or put apart (separation): *Mark separated the apples from the pears.*

separate (say <u>sep</u>rit) divided, not joined together

September the ninth month of the year

serious not playful or laughing

sermon a speech given by a minister of religion as part of a religious service

serve to work for or wait upon (servant, service)

settee a large comfortable seat for more than one person

settle 1. to arrange or decide upon: *Mary settled the date of her wedding next year.*
2. to come to rest or make a permanent home (settler): *Bill and June settled in Australia.*
3. to make full payment for: *Ken settled the bill for the repairs.*

several some of an uncertain number

severe 1. pitiless, stern: *The judge gave the prisoner a severe warning.*
2. harsh, painful: *Fiona had a severe pain in her stomach.*

sew to fasten with needle and thread (sewing)

shabby faded and worn out

shade 1. to shelter or protect from light or heat (shadow): *Amy shaded her face with a sun hat.*
2. a tone or hue or colour: *Peter painted a picture in different shades of green.*

DICTIONARY 147

S

shake/shook to tremble or shiver

shallow not deep

shame to make ashamed or sorry about something

shampoo to wash the hair with a soapy liquid

shape to mould or make into a particular form

share to divide among others

shark a very large fish with sharp teeth

sharp having a keen cutting edge or fine point

shatter to break into small pieces

shave to remove hair from the face of a man

shawl a piece of material worn around the shoulders

sheaf a bundle of stalks of wheat or other grain

shear to clip or cut with large scissors

sheath a close–fitting cover for a knife or sword

shed a small wooden house or hut

sheep a farm animal with soft, fleecy wool

sheer 1. to move away or swerve to the side: *The pony sheered away from the jump.*
2. very steep: *The drop from the top of the cliff to the rocks below was sheer.*
3. complete or absolute: *The children's faces shone from sheer pleasure.*

sheet 1. a thin flat piece of metal, cloth or paper
2. a broad expanse of water

sheik an Arab chief

148 **DICTIONARY**

shelf a board fixed to a wall

shell the hard outer covering of many animals, eggs and nuts

shelter to protect from danger or weather

shepherd a person who looks after sheep

shield 1. to protect from harm: *Sally shielded her face from the sun.*
2. a broad piece of armour carried on the arm to protect the wearer

shift to change the position or move

shin the front part of the leg, between the ankle and the knee

shine/shone to give out or reflect light

ship a vessel used to carry goods and passengers by sea

shipwreck a ship that has been totally destroyed by being driven onto the rocks

shirt a thin cotton or linen garment worn on the upper part of the body

shiver to shake or tremble

shoal 1. a large number of fish swimming together

2. a sandbank or shallow part of water

shock to give someone an unpleasant surprise or fright

shoe a covering for the foot

shoot/shot 1. to let off a gun or arrow: *Neil shot three arrows at the target.*
2. to sprout or grow from the tip: *The plants began to shoot up in the spring.*
3. to move swiftly and suddenly: *At the beginning of the race, Roger shot away from the other competitors.*

shop a building where goods are sold to the public (shopping)

shore the land at the edge of the sea

short not tall or long in space or time

DICTIONARY 149

S

shorts short trousers with legs that finish well above the knee

shoulder the joint which connects the arm to the body

shout to cry out loudly

shove to push against

shovel to lift or move with a broad spade

show to present to view or exhibit; to point to or prove

shower a fall of rain that is soon over

shriek to scream from fright

shrill make a loud high sound

shrink/shrank 1. to become smaller: *Jill's new sweater shrank in the wash.*
2. to draw back from: *The child shrank away from the snake on the ground.*

shrivel to dry up and become wrinkled

shrub a bushy low-growing plant with branches that grow from the root or from the stem just above the ground

shrug to raise the shoulders to show indifference or disdain

shudder to tremble with fear or horror

shuffle 1. to scrape the feet along the ground: *Amy shuffled through the dry leaves on the ground.*
2. to mix up the cards in a pack: *Jim shuffled the cards before they played snap.*

shut to close or fasten

shutter an outer window usually made of wood

shy timid or easily frightened

sick unwell

side an inner or outer surface or an edge of something

150 DICTIONARY

siege the surrounding of a town by an attacking army

siesta an afternoon sleep

sieve to sift or strain through a wire mesh

sigh to take a deep breath when tired or sad

sight the power of seeing or the thing seen

sign 1. to make a movement or gesture with the hand or head: *Bob signed to the children to keep quiet.* 2. to write your name (signature) 3. a notice that gives directions: *James looked out for the signs to London.*

signal to send a message

significant having a special meaning or importance

silence to stop making sounds or speech

silk a soft material made from thread produced by a silk-worm

sill the bottom ledge of a window

silly foolish, without sense

silver a shiny white metal dug from the ground

similar like, nearly the same

simmer to boil gently and slowly

simple not difficult; plain

since after that time

sincerity honest and truthful (sincere)

sing/sang to make musical sounds with the voice (singer, song)

singe to burn slightly on the surface

single one only

sinister evil-looking

S

sink/sank 1. to go down gradually in water: *The ship sank during the storm.*
2. a bowl fixed in a kitchen for washing dishes

siren a whistle or hooter on a ship blown to warn of danger

sister 1. a female whose parents are the same as another person
2. a nun
3. a nurse in a hospital

site to place in position

situate to put in a particular place (situation)

size bulk or bigness

skate 1. to glide over ice wearing boots with metal runners fixed to the soles (skater)

2. a large flat fish

skateboard a board with wheels underneath which is used for balancing tricks

skeleton the bony framework of a body

sketch to draw the outlines of a picture

ski to move over snow with long flat runners strapped to the feet (skier)

skid to slide sideways

skill cleverness in doing something (skilful)

skim to take off from the surface of a liquid

skin to take off the outer covering of an animal, fish or fruit

skip to jump over lightly (skipping)

skirt 1. the lower part of a woman's dress below the waist
2. to go around the edge of: *The path skirted the edge of the lake.*

skull the bony part of the head

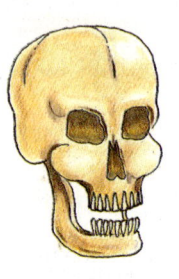

S

sky the upper atmosphere as seen from the Earth

skylight a small window in the roof of a house

skyscraper a very tall building

slab a thick flat piece of anything

slack loose

slam to shut noisily and violently

slant to give a slope to

slap to hit with an open hand

slash to cut through with a knife

slaughter to kill

slave a servant who is not given any money to work

slay/slew to kill

sledge to ride on a sort of carriage with runners for gliding over snow

sleep/slept to take a rest and close the eyes

sleet a mixture of snow and rain falling at the same time

sleeve the part of a garment that covers the arm

sleigh a horse-drawn sledge

slender thin or narrow

slice to cut off thin flat pieces

slide/slid to move smoothly

slight light, little, unimportant

slim to reduce one's weight by dieting

sling/slung 1. a weapon for throwing stones
2. a support for an injured arm
3. to throw with a swinging motion of the arm

slink/slunk to move in a stealthy way

slip 1. to slide and fall: *Jean slipped and fell on the ice*
2. to move away or escape: *The dog slipped out of the room.*
3. to move something quickly and secretly: *The boy slipped the envelope into his pocket.*

DICTIONARY 153

S

slipper a loose, comfortable shoe worn indoors

slit 1. to cut open: *Bill slit open the envelope.* 2. a narrow opening or cut: *The dog escaped through a slit in the fence.*

slither to slip and slide on a slippery surface

slope to put something at an angle or on a slant

slot a slit where coins are put into automatic machines to make them work

slow not swift or fast

slug a kind of snail without a shell

slum a dirty overcrowded run-down part of a town

slumber to sleep

slush wet, half-melted snow mixed with mud

sly untruthful and deceitful

smack to hit with the open hand

small little in size, number or amount

smart 1. to feel a sharp stinging pain 2. well-dressed and neat looking

smash 1. to break into pieces: *The cup smashed into pieces when it fell on the floor.* 2. a car accident: *Luckily, Henry was not hurt in the smash.*

smear to rub over with a greasy or oily substance and leave a mark or coating

smell/smelt to detect an odour or perfume with the nose

smile to show pleasure or amusement by a curve of the lips

smoke to give out a cloudy mass as a result of burning something

154 DICTIONARY

smooth to make flat and even

smother to suffocate or cut off the supply of air

smoulder to burn slowly without making a flame

smudge to make a dirty mark

smuggle to bring goods secretly into a country without paying taxes to the government (smuggler)

smut a spot of dirt

snack a light meal

snag 1. to catch on something: *John's jersey snagged on the barbed wire.*
2. a problem or difficulty: *The snag was Julie had to get up very early to catch her plane.*

snail a slow-moving, slimy creature with a shell on its back

snake a reptile with a smooth scaly skin, a long body and no arms or legs

snap 1. to bite quickly: *The puppy snapped up the piece of sandwich that fell on the ground.*
2. to break or crack: *Henry snapped the biscuit in half.*
3. speak in a short sharp way: *Jack snapped at his wife when she asked him a question.*

snare to trap animals

snarl to growl like an angry dog

snatch to grab or seize quickly

sneak to creep or steal away; to do mean or unpleasant things

sneer to make cutting remarks about a person

sneeze to blow out air suddenly through the nose

sniff to draw in breath through the nose with a sharp hiss

snip to cut off with scissors (snippet)

snivel to have a runny nose

DICTIONARY 155

S

snooze to doze or sleep for a short time

snore to breathe noisily through an open mouth when asleep

snort to make an angry noise through the nose

snout the long nose of an animal

snow to fall or cover with white flakes of frozen rain

snug warm and comfortable

soak to make or get very wet

soap a fatty substance used for washing

soar to fly up high in the air

sober not drunk; calm and sensible

soccer association football

society people living or associating together (social, sociable)

sock a warm covering for the foot worn under a shoe

sodden very wet

sofa a long soft seat

soft not hard, but yielding when touched

soil 1. earth in which plants grow
2. to make dirty

solar connected with the Sun

soldier a person who is a member of an army

sole 1. one and only: *Kate was the sole survivor of the crash.*
2. a kind of flat fish

solemn very serious

solid not hollow; not liquid or gas

solitary living alone; lonely

solo something played or sung by one person

156 DICTIONARY

solve to find an answer to a problem (solution)

somersault to turn head over heels

son a male child

soon in a short time

soot a black dust caused by smoke from a fire

soothe to calm down or quieten

sorcerer a magician

sore painful

sorrow sadness

sort to divide up by the kind or class

sound 1. to make a noise: *The cathedral bells sounded very loud.* 2. in good condition: *We all got home safe and sound.*

soup a liquid food made by boiling meat or vegetables

sour having an unpleasant, acid taste

source the starting point e.g. of a stream

south the region or point below the equator

souvenir an item that reminds you of a place, a person or a particular time.

sow to plant seeds in the soil

space 1. to place at the same distance apart: *The runners spaced themselves out before the race.* 2. the heavens: *The rocket lifted the spacecraft into space.*

3. an open place with plenty of room: *There was plenty of space to play games in the garden.*

spade a long-handled tool for digging

spaghetti a kind of long pasta or macaroni

spank to strike a child with the flat of the hand (spanking)

DICTIONARY 157

S

spare 1. left over, unwanted, extra: *Martin had a spare room in his house.*
2. to give away or do without: *Jean could not spare any money for a holiday.*
3. to show mercy to: *The king spared the life of the criminal.*

sparkle to make a quick flash of light (spark)

sparrow a small, brown garden bird

spawn to cast the eggs of fish or frogs

speak/spoke to talk about (speaker, speech)

spear a long–handled weapon with a sharp point

special intended for a particular use; not general

specimen an example or sample

speck a very small spot or bit of something

spectator a person who watches but does not take part in a show, games, etc.

speed quickness of movement

speedometer an instrument to measure speed

spell 1. to name the letters that make up a word (spelling)
2. a magic charm
3. a period of time: *Ben had a spell on the climbing frame.*

spend/spent 1. to use money for buying things: *Jane spent her money on new clothes.*
2. to pass a certain amount of time: *Ian spent most of his time reading books.*

sphere a round solid body or ball

sphinx a carved figure with a woman's head and a lion's body

spice a powder which adds taste and smell to food

158 DICTIONARY

spider a small animal with eight legs which spins webs to catch insects

spill to allow liquid to run out accidentally

spin/spun 1. to turn round and round: *Wendy spun a coin to see who would start the game.*
2. to make thread from cotton or wool fibres

spine the backbone of the body

spiral a round, twisted shape like a corkscrew

spire the tall pointed part of a church steeple

spirit 1. a ghost
2. an alcoholic drink
3. a mood or feeling: *Ted was in very good spirits when he passed his exam.*

spit/spat to throw saliva out of the mouth

spite an unkind wish to harm someone (spiteful)

splash to spatter water about

splint a piece of wood tied with a bandage to a broken limb to help it heal correctly

splinter a small sharp piece of wood, metal or glass

split to divide up into parts

spoil to do harm or damage

sponge 1. to wash lightly with the soft remains of a sea animal: *Martha sponged the baby in the bath.*

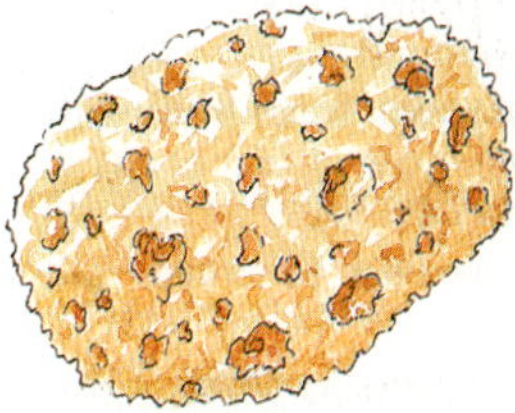

2. a light, soft cake: *Mother made a sponge cake for tea.*

DICTIONARY 159

S

spoon a table utensil with a shallow bowl at one end of the handle

sport games played in the open air; fun and amusement

spot 1. to see something: *James tried to spot his friend in the crowd.*
2. a small mark: *Bill had a painful spot on his nose.*
3. a place: *We found a pleasant spot by the river for our picnic.*

spout to flow out from a pipe or tube

sprain to injure a limb by twisting it

spray to sprinkle with a shower of fine drops of water

spread to stretch out or cover a surface with

spring/sprang 1. to leap or jump up
2. the place where water comes out of the ground at the start of a river
3. one of the four seasons of the year
4. a coiled up wire

sprout to begin to grow

squabble to argue or quarrel with

squad a small party of people at work

squall a sudden storm or shower of rain

squander to spend money foolishly; to waste

square a shape with four equal sides and four corners that are at right angles

squash 1. to flatten or crush: *Martha squashed the beetle under her foot.*
2. a drink made of squeezed fruit juices

squawk to make a shrill, harsh cry

squeak to make a small high sound

squeal to make a long shrill sound of pain or pleasure

squeeze to press or crush between two things

squint to look with the eyes turned in different directions

squirm to wriggle or twist

squirrel a small tree–living rodent with a long fluffy tail

stab to cut or wound with a pointed instrument

S

stable a building where horses are kept

stack to pile up in a heap

stadium a large sports ground with seats around it

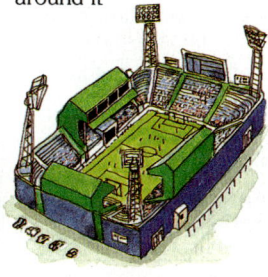

staff a group of people working together in a business, shop or school

stag a male deer

stage a raised wooden platform in a theatre or hall

stagger to walk unsteadily as if about to fall

stagnate to stop flowing and become foul

stain to make a dirty mark

stair one of a series of steps leading to an upper or lower floor in a building

stale not fresh

stalk 1. to steal up on animals quietly: *Mac stalked the stag on the hillside.* 
2. the stem of a leaf or plant

stall 1. a division in a stable for a single animal
2. a stand or booth in a market place 
3. a seat in the front rows of a theatre
4. to stop an engine running by mistake: *Ken stalled the car on the hill.*

stammer to talk with hesitation or difficulty

DICTIONARY 161

S

stamp 1. to strike the ground heavily with one foot: *The child stamped her foot in rage.*
2. to put a postage stamp on a letter

stand/stood 1. to remain upright, not seated: *The children all stood when the head teacher came into the room.*
2. to remain in position and not run away or move: *Susan stood her ground even though she was afraid of the lion.*

star a bright light in the sky at night

starboard the right side of the ship when facing forwards

starch 1. a white, floury food substance found in bread and potatoes
2. to make cloth stiff

stare to look at long and hard

starfish a flat sea animal with five arms

start 1. to begin: *In the afternoon it started to rain.*
2. to make a sudden jump for fear or surprise: *Ann started when she saw the mouse.*

starve to suffer or die from hunger (starvation)

station 1. to put in position: *Mary stationed herself near the window.*
2. a building where trains depart and arrive

stationary staying in one place and not moving

stationery paper, pencils and other materials for writing

statue a carved figure made of wood, stone or metal

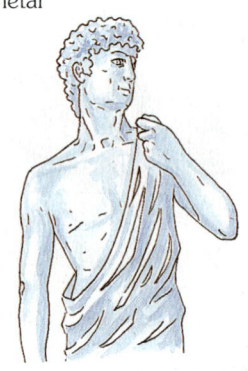

stay to remain in a place and not move away

steak a thick slice of meat or fish

162 DICTIONARY

steal/stole to take something that belongs to another person

steam fine drops of vapour from boiling water

steel a strong metal made by heating iron and carbon

steep 1. a slope at a sharp angle: *The path up the hill was very steep.*
2. to soak in water: *She steeped the shirt in soapy water to get rid of the stains.*

steeple the tall tower of a church

steer to make a boat, car or plane move in a certain direction (steering)

stem the straight part of a plant above ground that bears the flowers and leaves

step to put one foot in front of the other

stern 1. the back end of a boat
2. serious and strict: *Bob's dad was very strict and stern.*

stew to cook meat slowly with vegetables in one pot

stick/stuck 1. to fix with a pin or paste: *Peter stuck the notice on the wall.*
2. a small branch from a tree or shrub: *Judy threw a stick for the dog to fetch.*

stiff not easily bent or moved

stile steps to help people climb over a fence or wall

still 1. quiet and peaceful, without movement: *The water was so still we could see every ripple.*
2. up to this time; yet: *James was still hungry after the meal.*

DICTIONARY 163

S

sting to prick and cause a sharp pain

stir 1. to mix with a spoon: *Pam stirred the milk into the flour.*
2. to move: *Henry told the children not to stir from their seats.*

stirrup a metal loop on a strap for supporting the foot of a horse rider

stitch to sew together

stocking a long close-fitting covering to keep the leg warm

stomach an organ inside the body where food is digested

stone a lump of rock

stool a seat with no back to lean against

stop 1. to bring to a halt or prevent movement: *Fred stopped the car near the post office.*
2. not to continue in an action: *Lucy stopped biting her nails.*

store 1. to keep things together for future use: *Ben stored up his sweets until the weekend.*
2. a large shop

storey a set of rooms in a building that are on one floor

stork a large bird with long legs and a long beak

storm bad weather, with thunder and lightning

story a tale or history of events

straight not crooked or bent

strain 1. to stretch or make a great effort: *The dog strained against the lead.*
2. to pass through a sieve: *Mother strained the tea-leaves.*

strange 1. odd or unusual: *The cat was making strange sounds*
2. unknown or not seen before (stranger)

164 DICTIONARY

strangle to choke by holding tightly around the neck (strangler)

strap a narrow band of leather

straw a stalk of corn after the grain has been thrashed out

strawberry a juicy red berry with a sweet taste

stray to wander from the path and get lost

stream a small river

street a road with houses on either side

strength full of power; difficult to break (strong)

stretch 1. to make longer or wider by pulling out: *Kate's jumper stretched when she washed it.*
2. to hold or reach out: *The baby stretched out to touch the toy.*

stretcher a frame covered with canvas to carry a sick person

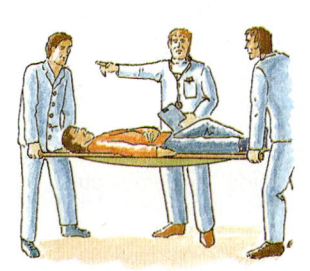

strict paying great attention to the rules

strike/struck 1. to hit a person or thing: *Tom struck the ball as hard as he could.*
2. to stop work because of an argument with the management of the company: *The workers went on strike for more pay.*

string very thin rope or cord

strip 1. to pull or tear off, to take the covering off: *Judy stripped off the paper around the flowers.*
2. to undress: *Neil stripped off his clothes and jumped into the water.*
3. a long thin piece of paper or cloth

DICTIONARY 165

S

stripe a narrow line or band of different colour

stroke to pass the hand gently over

stroll to walk slowly and leisurely from place to place

struggle to fight against

stubborn obstinate, with a fixed opinion

studio a room where an artist or photographer works

study to learn about different subjects and gain knowledge (student)

stuff to fill a cushion, etc. with bits of material

stuffy hot and airless

stumble to trip and almost fall

stun to make unconscious by a blow or shock

stupid foolish, not clever

stutter to speak with difficulty

sty a shed for pigs

style a fashion or way of doing things (stylish)

subject (say sub<u>j</u>ekt) to bring under the power or control of (subject, say <u>sub</u>jekt)

submarine a warship which travels under the sea

submerge to put under water; to cover with water

submit to surrender or give way (submission)

substance the stuff or material of which a thing is made

substitute to put in place of another person or thing (substitution)

subterranean underground

subtract to take away from (subtraction)

suburb the outer part of a town or city between the town and country (suburban)

166 DICTIONARY

S

subway an underground passage

succeed 1. to follow after or take the place of (succession): *Peter succeeded Tom as head of school.*
2. to get on well and do what you wanted to do (success): *Kate succeeded in passing all her exams.*

suck to draw into the mouth; to soak up liquid

sudden happening without notice or warning

suffer to bear pain or punishment (sufferer, suffering)

suffocate to kill by choking off air (suffocation)

sugar a sweet substance made from cane or sugar beet.

suggest to bring forward an idea; to advise a person about something (suggestion)

suit 1. to be convenient or to please: *It suited John to go by car rather than by train.*
2. matching trousers and jacket: *Fred bought himself a new suit for the wedding.*

suitcase a box with a handle in which clothes are packed when travelling

sulk to be silent because in a bad temper

sullen gloomy, in a bad mood

sulphur a pale yellow substance which is not metallic

sultana a dried white grape

summary a short statement of facts in a few words

DICTIONARY 167

S

summer the warmest of the four seasons of the year

summit the highest point of a mountain

summon to call or send for (summons)

sun a very bright star that sends rays of heat and light to Earth

Sunday the first day of the week

sunflower a large yellow flower on a tall stem grown for its seeds

sunstroke an illness caused by too much exposure to the sun

superior higher in place, position or rank

supermarket a large shop where food is selected by customers from shelves

supervise to direct and control; to oversee (supervision)

supper a meal eaten in the evening

supple able to bend easily

supply to provide what is wanted

support to hold up

suppose to think or believe something to be true (supposition)

sure certain, without any doubt

surf the foam of waves breaking on the shore

surface the outside layer or skin

surgeon a doctor who performs operations in a hospital (surgery)

surname the family name

surplus what is left over and not needed

surprise to come upon unexpectedly; to astonish

surrender to stop fighting and give up or stop resisting

surround to be on all sides of (surroundings)

survey to look over or at

suspect (say sus<u>pekt</u>) to have a vague idea but no proof of wrong doing (suspect, say <u>sus</u>pekt; suspicion)

suspend to hang from above (suspension)

suspense a feeling of anxiety while waiting for news

swallow 1. to pass food and drink from the mouth into the stomach: *Betty swallowed her food quickly.*
2. a small bird that spends the summers in cool northern countries and winters in warmer countries

swamp a bog or marsh

swan a large bird with webbed feet for swimming, and a long graceful neck

swarm 1. to collect together in large numbers: *The fans swarmed to the rock concert.*
2. a mass of insects, such as bees or locusts

sway to move from side to side

swear/swore 1. to use bad language: *The postman swore when the dog bit him.*
2. to make a solemn promise: *Bill swore that he would always be my friend.*

sweat to perspire or have moisture appearing on the skin when too hot

sweater a warm knitted garment with long sleeves

sweep/swept 1. to brush away: *Jan swept up the broken glass on the floor.*
2. a person who cleans chimneys

S

sweet 1. pleasant to taste, smell or hear 2. a pudding, or something made of sugar

swell to increase in size or get larger (swelling)

swerve to move suddenly to one side

swift 1. quick: *Jan made a swift movement of her head.* 2. a small bird like a swallow

swim/swam to move through the water using arms and legs (swimming)

swindle to cheat or get dishonestly

swing/swung to move backwards and forwards, to and fro

switch 1. to turn electric current off or on: *Jean switched on the lights when it got dark.* 2. to move from one thing to another: *Jon switched his studies from a history degree to a science degree.*

sword a weapon with a long flat metal blade and sharp edges

sympathy a kind feeling for someone who is in trouble (sympathetic)

symptom a sign of illness

syrup a sweet, sugary liquid

system a well thought out plan or method (systematic)

T

table 1. a piece of furniture with a smooth flat surface supported by four legs 2. a systematic arrangement of figures or facts (multiplication table)

tablet 1. a slab of stone fixed to a wall with writing on it 2. a small pill of medicine

tack 1. to fasten with long loose stitches: *Wendy tacked up the hem of her new skirt.* 2. to fasten by hammering in small sharp pointed nails: *Roger tacked the notice to the wall.* 3. to change the direction of a sailing ship by moving the sails 4. the saddle, bridle etc. for a horse

170 DICTIONARY

tackle 1. to try to do something difficult: *Sarah tackled the more difficult side of the mountain.*
2. to try to take the ball away from the other side during a match

3. equipment or tools needed to do something (fishing tackle)

tadpole the stage between the egg and the adult frog

tail the long flexible end of an animal's spine; the back end of anything

tailor a person who makes men's clothes

take/took to seize or hold; to choose or select; to remove

tale a story

talent the ability to do something well

talk to speak and discuss

tall high, not short or low

talon the hooked claw of a bird of prey

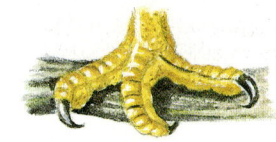

tame to make a wild animal obey; to domesticate

tangerine a small, sweet kind of orange

tangle to twist up

tank 1. a large basin or box for holding liquid (fish tank)
2. an armed vehicle that can move over rough ground

DICTIONARY 171

T

tape 1. a narrow piece of woven material
2. a measure of length marked with divisions at intervals (tape measure)
3. a magnetic strip on which music or sounds are recorded (tape recorder)

tapestry a heavy cloth with embroidered scenes worked on it

tar a thick, black sticky liquid used to bind stones together on the surface of a road

target a mark to aim at in a shooting practice

tart 1. an open, flat pie filled with fruit
2. having a sharp, bitter taste

tartan woollen cloth woven with a pattern of stripes crossing over each other

task a job that has to be done

taste to test the flavour of food or drink with the tongue

tattoo 1. to make the sound of a beating drum
2. to make a pattern or picture in a person's skin with needles and colours

taxi a motor car which people hire to take them somewhere

tea a drink made by pouring boiling water onto dried leaves from the tea-plant, a small shrub grown in hot countries

teach/taught to show or tell a person how to do something (teacher)

team a group of people all doing or working at the same thing

tear/tore (say tair) to pull apart or pull to pieces

tear (say teer) a small drop of water from the eye

tease to annoy or make fun of

teddy-bear a stuffed, cuddly toy bear

172 DICTIONARY

T

telephone an electrical instrument which people use to speak to each other at a distance

telescope an instrument which makes it possible to see things a long way off

television an electrical instrument which receives pictures transmitted from a distance

tell/told to say or inform

temper an attitude or feeling, whether good or bad

temperate neither too hot nor too cold

temperature how hot or cold a thing is

tempest a violent wind storm

temple a building used for worship

temporary lasting for only a short time

tempt to persuade someone to do wrong

tend 1. to look after or take care of: *The shepherd tended the sheep on the hills.*
2. to be likely to (tendency): *Too much chocolate and sweets tends to make you fat.*

tender 1. easily harmed or hurt: *The baby had a soft, tender skin.*
2. soft and well cooked: *The stew was very tender after three hours in the oven.*
3. gentle and kind

tennis a ball game played with stringed rackets on a large court

tent a temporary shelter made of poles and canvas, fastened with ropes

tepid cool, not too warm

DICTIONARY 173

T

term a fixed period of time

terminus the end of a railway or bus route

terrace 1. a raised lawn or paved area beside a house
2. a row of houses joined together

terrific huge and impressive

terror great fear or horror (terrible)

test to examine or try out

tether to tie with a rope

text the words of a speech or in a book

thank to say how grateful you are

thatch to cover a building with a roof of straw or rushes

thaw to warm up or melt

theatre a building where plays, concerts and shows are put on

thermometer an instrument to measure the amount of heat or cold

thick dense, not thin

thicket a place where shrubs and trees grow very close together

thief a person who steals from another (thieves, theft)

thigh the thick part of the leg between the hip and the knee

thimble a small cap worn on the finger when sewing

thin having little depth or thickness; slim

think/thought to reason, to imagine or have an opinion

thirst to need or want a drink

thistle a prickly plant with a purple flower

thorn a sharp point or prickle on the stem of some plants

thousand ten hundred (1,000)

thread a thin, strong twist of wool, cotton or silk used for sewing

threaten to promise to punish or do harm to (threat)

thresh to beat the grain out of corn

thrill to feel pleasure or excitement

throat the front part of the neck

throb to beat strongly and regularly

throne a special seat for a king or queen

throttle 1. to choke or cut off the air: *Sue's necklace was so tight, it nearly throttled her.*
2. the part of a machine that increases the speed of the engine: *Dad put his foot down on the throttle and the car gathered speed.*

through from end to end of; going in at one side and out the other

throw/threw to fling or hurl something a distance away

thrush a small song bird with a spotted breast

thud a dull sound made by a blow or heavy fall

thumb the short thick finger on the hand

thump to knock or give a heavy blow

thunder the noise in the sky that comes after a flash of lightning during a storm

Thursday the fifth day of the week

tick 1. to make a small mark beside something: *The teacher ticked all the answers.*
2. the noise made by a clock when it is beating
3. a small blood-sucking insect

T

ticket a small piece of paper or card giving the owner the right to travel on a train, plane or bus or attend a concert, etc.

tickle to touch the skin lightly and make someone laugh

tide the regular movement of the sea up and down the beach under the influence of the moon

tidy neat and in good order

tie to join together the ends of a rope or cord; to fasten

tiger a large wild animal like a cat with a striped coat

tighten to make something fit very closely

tile to cover with small thin plates of baked clay

till 1. to plough the earth and sow seeds 2. the machine a shopkeeper uses to keep money

tiller the bar used as a lever to turn the rudder to steer a boat

timber trees that have been cut down

time a period or moment; the past present and future

timid shy, not very brave

tingle to feel a faint prickling sensation in the skin

tinkle to make a small, high ringing sound

tint to add colour

tiny very small

tire to become weary or exhausted

title 1. the name of a book, play or poem 2. a name showing rank

toadstool a fungus like a mushroom, often poisonous

toast to heat a slice of bread and make both sides brown

tobacco the dried leaves of a plant that are used for smoking cigarettes and pipes

T

toboggan a kind of sledge used to slide down snow-covered hillsides

today this day; at the present time

toe one of the five small joints at the end of the foot

toffee a sweet made by boiling sugar and butter together

toilet washing and dressing or going to the lavatory

tomato a round, red juicy salad vegetable

tomorrow the day after today

tone the sound of a voice or musical instrument

tongue the flexible muscle inside the mouth used for tasting and swallowing

tonight this night

tool a thing which helps one do or make something

tooth one of the hard white objects inside the mouth used to crush up food (teeth)

topple to fall over

torch a light that can be carried in the hand

tornado a violent wind storm which travels at great speed

torpedo a cigar-shaped underwater explosive weapon of war

torrent a very fast flowing river

tortoise a toothless reptile with a dome-shaped shell

torture to deliberately cause very great pain

toss to throw up into the air

DICTIONARY 177

T

total to add up all the numbers; a complete number

totter to walk unsteadily

touch to feel with the hand

tough hard, strong

tour to travel from one place to another (tourist)

tournament a sports competition

tow to pull along behind; to drag through the water

towards in the direction of

towel a fluffy cloth used to dry the body after washing

tower to reach up into the sky

town a collection of houses in one place

toy a child's plaything

track 1. to follow the trail: *Dave tracked the animal for a long time.* 2. a rough path: *The track through the woods was very overgrown.*

tracksuit a warm suit worn over sporting clothes after a competition

tractor an engine on wheels used to pull heavy loads

trade to buy and sell goods (trader)

traffic the general movement of people or vehicles to and fro

tragedy a story or play with a sad ending

trail to follow the track of; to draw or drag along the ground (trailer)

train 1. to teach a person how to do something: *Jane's teacher trained her to write neatly.*
2. a railway engine and coaches

traitor a person who gives secret information to the enemy

tramp 1. to walk heavily: *Henry tramped along the path.*
2. a person who has no permanent home but wanders from place to place

trample to tread heavily underfoot

transatlantic crossing or across the Atlantic Ocean

transfer to move from one place or person to another

transform to change completely (transformation)

translate to change words and sentences in one language into another language (translator, translation)

transparent anything that can be easily seen through

transplant to take up and plant in another place

transport to move or carry from one place to another

trap to catch so that the object can move no longer (trapper)

trapeze a swinging bar on which acrobats do tricks

travel to go from one place to another (traveller)

trawler a fishing boat which pulls nets along the sea bed

tray a flat piece of metal or wood used to carry plates of food

treacle a sweet, thick, sugary liquid

tread to walk or move carefully

treason disloyalty or treachery by a traitor

DICTIONARY 179

T

treasure 1. a collection of valuable things: *The pirates buried their treasure on the island.*

2. to look after very carefully: *Amy treasured the letter from her father.*

treat 1. to behave towards someone or something in a certain way (treatment): *Ken treated all his friends with disdain.*
2. a pleasure: *Jenny gave each child a chocolate as a treat.*
3. to cure an illness: *The doctor treated Tom for his ear–ache.*

tree a large plant with a thick, woody trunk and many branches

tremble to shiver or shake from fear or cold (trembling)

trench a long narrow ditch or hole in the ground

trespass to go where it is forbidden (trespasser)

trial a legal test in a court of law

triangle a figure with three sides and three angles

tribe a group of people who are descended from the same ancestor (tribal)

trick to play a joke on or deceive

trickle to flow out very slowly in small drops

tricycle a bicycle with three wheels

trip a short journey by sea or land

troop to move together in one mass or body

tropics the hot part of the world just north or south of the equator

trot to move with short, quick steps

trouble to bother, annoy or worry

trough a long, open vessel for holding water or food for animals

trousers a garment that covers the lower part of the body and each leg

trowel a small hand spade used by gardeners

180 DICTIONARY

truce an agreement between enemies to stop fighting for a short time

truck a small lorry; an open, uncovered railway wagon

trudge to plod or walk wearily

true correct, not a lie or false (truth)

trumpet a metal musical instrument which is played by blowing into it

trunk 1. the main part of a tree between the branches and the roots
2. the long nose of an elephant
3. a large box for carrying or storing clothes

trust to have confidence or faith in

try/tried to test or attempt to do something

tube a hollow length of material

tuft a bunch of something soft, ie. hair, wool or grass.

tulip a colourful spring flower that grows from a bulb

tumble to fall heavily

tune a series of musical notes, a melody

tunnel an underground passage cut through a hill or under a town or river

turban a long strip of material wound around the head

turf surface soil which contains the matted roots of grass

turkey a large fowl bred for its meat

turn to move around, to change position or direction (turning)

turnip a root vegetable with a hard white flesh

DICTIONARY 181

T

turret a small tower on a building

turtle a sea animal like a large tortoise

tusk a long tooth which sticks out

twig a small branch

twilight the half light after the sun sets before it gets completely dark

twin one of two children born at the same time to the same mother; one thing that is exactly like another

twinkle to sparkle and shine brightly

twist to turn around; to wind together

type 1. a kind or sort: *Some types of animals sleep all winter.* 2. to write or print words and letters on a typewriter

typhoon a violent storm that happens in the Far East

tyre the outer rubber tube of a car or bicycle wheel

U

udder the organ that holds the milk of cows and goats

ugly unpleasant to look at

umbrella a round piece of lightweight material stretched over a frame to keep the rain off

umpire to watch the players in a game and make sure the rules are obeyed

uncle the brother of one's father or mother

under below, beneath the surface

underground under the surface of the ground

understand/understood to know the meaning of, or know all about (understanding)

undertake to agree to do (undertaking)

182 DICTIONARY

V

uneasy anxious, worried

uniform the clothes worn by all the members of a group

unite to join together and make into one (union)

universe the whole world (universal)

unkind cruel and heartless

unpleasant nasty, disagreeable

untidy messy, in great disorder

unusual out of the ordinary, uncommon

upright standing straight up

upset 1. to spill or knock over: *Jane upset her glass of lemonade all over the table.* 2. to make ill or unhappy: *Wendy was upset that she could not go to the party.*

upside-down with the upper side underneath

vacate to leave empty or unoccupied (vacancy)

vacation a holiday

vaccinate to give a person an injection to prevent them catching a disease (vaccination)

vague uncertain, not sure

vain 1. proud of one's personal appearance: *May was very vain about her good looks.* 2. useless: *Bill looked everywhere for his lost ticket, but all in vain.*

valley a lower area of land between two hills or mountains

value 1. to hold in respect and admiration: *Ken valued Joan's opinion of his work.* 2. the price or worth of something (valuation): *Penny tried to guess the value of the necklace.*

DICTIONARY 183

V

vampire a make believe person that leaves the grave at night to suck blood from sleepers

vanish to disappear

various of many kinds

varnish to paint with a clear liquid that dries to give a hard, shiny finish

vary to change or make different (variety)

vase a container for holding cut flowers

vast huge, enormous

vegetable a plant that can be eaten with the meat course

vegetarian a person who eats no animal flesh

vehicle anything that carries or moves things from one place to another

veil a piece of thin, transparent material to cover the face

ventilate to let fresh air in (ventilation)

verdict a judgement, the decision of the judge or jury after a trial

vermin harmful animals

version a story with a different point of view or opinion to the original story

vertebrate having a backbone

vertical straight up and down

vessel 1. a container for liquid
2. a ship or boat

veto to say no to something, to forbid

vex to annoy or make angry

viaduct a high bridge or series of arches to carry a road or railway over a valley

venom poison (venomous)

vibrate to move to and fro, to quiver (vibration)

V

vice 1. a wicked habit (vicious): *James was a person with no vices.* 2. an instrument with two jaws to grip things tightly

vicinity the neighbourhood or district

victim a person who suffers from the action of others

victory the defeat of an army or of an opponent or competitor (victorious)

video a magnetic tape recorded with programmes that can be seen on a television set when played through a video machine

view 1. to look at or see: *James viewed the photograph album with interest.* 2. what can be seen, scenery: *I had a view over the lake from my windows.* 3. opinion: *Nick's view was that playing football was a waste of time.*

vigour strength and energy (vigorous)

vile evil, horrible

village a small group of houses in the country

villain a wicked person, one who does wrong (villainous)

vine a climbing plant from which grapes grow

vinegar a sour, acid liquid

violence rough or cruel behaviour that can harm others (violent)

violet 1. a purplish-blue colour
2. a small purple flower

violin a musical instrument with strings which is played with a bow (violinist)

viper a small, poisonous snake

visible able to be seen

vision 1. the power of seeing
2. an imaginary sight

DICTIONARY 185

V

visit to go or come to see a person (visitor)

vital necessary to life; very important

vivid bright and clear

voice the sounds made through the mouth when speaking, singing or shouting (vocal)

volcano a mountain that throws out dust and molten rocks or lava (volcanic)

volunteer to offer to do something of your own free will

vote to express what you want by marking a piece of paper or by a show of hands (voter)

vow a solemn promise

voyage to travel across the sea

vulture a large ugly bird that feeds on the flesh of dead animals

W

waddle to walk like a duck with short steps and swaying from side to side

wade to walk in shallow water

wag to shake from side to side

wage the money earned by doing a job

wagon a heavy four-wheeled cart to carry goods

wail to cry out in sorrow

waist the narrowest part of the body above the hips and below the ribs

wait to stay in one place until another person arrives (waiter)

wake/woke to come out of sleep

walk to take steps forward slowly

W

wall the side of a building or an enclosure made of brick or stone

wallet a small leather folder for holding money and papers

walnut a nut with a hard crinkled shell

walrus a large sea animal with tusks

waltz to dance to music with a three-four beat

wand a long, thin stick used by a conjurer or magician

wander to ramble here and there without a fixed plan

wane to become smaller

want to wish, desire or need

war armed conflict between two enemies (warrior)

wardrobe a cupboard for hanging up clothes

warm to heat up but not make too hot

warn to advise against (warning)

warren underground burrows where rabbits live

wart a small, hard lump on the skin

wary cautious, watching out for danger

wash to clean with soap and water (washing)

wasp a stinging insect with a striped body

waste to use foolishly and without care

watch 1. to look at: *Susan watched the ducks feeding in the pond.*
2. a small clock worn on the wrist

water a transparent, tasteless liquid that falls as rain

waterfall the place where a stream or river falls over a ledge

waterproof material that does not allow water to soak in

DICTIONARY 187

W

wave 1. to move something up and down: *The children waved flags during the queen's visit.*
2. the movement of water on the surface of the sea

wax 1. a yellow substance made by bees to build a honeycomb
2. to increase in size: *The moon waxed and waned.*

way 1. a path or road: *Roger asked the way to the library.*
2. a method or habit: *Jim knew the way to look after goldfish.*

weaken to make less strong (weakness)

wealth an amount of money and riches

weapon an instrument to fight with

wear/wore to have clothes on

weary tired

weasel a small, fierce animal with a long body and short legs that changes the colour of its coat to white in the winter

weather the condition of the atmosphere around us, whether hot or cold, wet or dry, cloudy or sunny

weave to make cloth by crossing threads over and under each other (weaver)

wed to marry (wedding)

Wednesday the fourth day of the week

weed to pull up wild, unwanted plants growing in the garden

week the period of seven days from Sunday to Saturday

weep/wept to cry and show grief (weeping)

weigh to find out how heavy something is (weight)

weird strange, unearthly

welcome to show pleasure when a person comes

west in the direction of the setting sun

whale the largest sea animal, warm–blooded and with lungs to breathe air

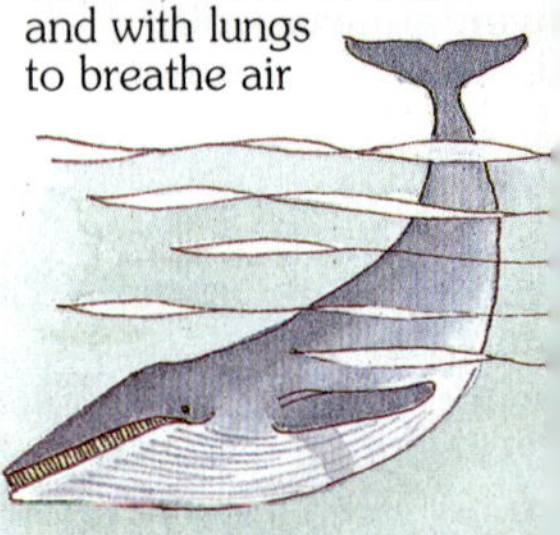

188 DICTIONARY

W

wharf a stone or timber structure where ships can tie up and unload

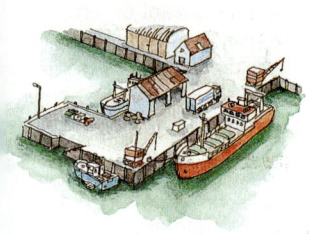

wheat a grain that is ground up to make flour

wheel a round frame that turns on a central axis

whimper to cry softly

whine to make an unhappy cry like a dog (whining)

whip to strike with a lash or leather thong

whirl to turn around quickly

whisker one of the long sensitive hairs on the nose of animals

whisper to speak in a very low voice

whistle to make a high sharp sound by blowing air through pursed lips

white with no colour

whole the complete amount or all

wicked evil, sinful

width the distance from one side to the other (wide)

widow a woman whose husband has died

wife a woman who is married (wives)

wig a covering for the head made of false hair

wigwam an American–Indian tent

wild living in a state of nature; not tame or domesticated

wilderness an area of land that has not been cultivated but left in its wild, natural state

willow a tree with long branches that bend easily

DICTIONARY 189

W

wind/wound (say <u>wined</u>) to twist around, to coil

wind (say <u>wind</u>) movement of the air

windmill a machine with huge arms or sails that are turned by the wind

window an opening in a wall to let in air and light

wine an alcoholic drink made from the juice of grapes

wing the part of the body that enables flight, such as the feathered arms of a bird

wink to close and open one eye quickly

winter the coldest season of the year (wintry)

wipe to rub over lightly to make clean and dry

wire a long, thin metal thread

wisdom having good sense and judgement (wise)

wish to want or long for

witch a woman who has magic powers to make spells

wither to fade and become dry

witness to say one has personal proof or knowledge of some event; to give evidence

wizard a man who has magic powers to make spells

wolf a large wild dog

woman an adult female human being

wonder to feel surprised or amazed

wood 1. the material from the stem and branches of a tree 2. a collection of trees growing in one place

wool 1. the hair that grows on the skin of a sheep or goat 2. the twisted thread made from sheep's hair (woollen)

190 DICTIONARY

word the spoken or written sign of an idea

work to do a job; to labour (worker)

world the earth and the people who live on it

worm a long, soft creature with a jointed body that lives in the earth and feeds on dead matter

worry to feel anxious and troubled

wound to injure and cause bleeding

wrap to put a cover around (wrapper)

wrath great anger

wreath a circle of flowers and leaves

wreck to destroy or ruin something

wrench to twist or force off violently

wrestle to struggle against (wrestler)

wrinkle to crease or make folds

wrist the joint between the arm and the hand

write to form letters and words on paper (writing)

wrong 1. incorrect, bad 2. to do an injury or injustice

X

X-ray a ray which can pass through soft tissue and make a photograph of hard tissue on a photographic plate

xylophone a musical instrument which makes different notes when a hammer strikes blocks of different lengths

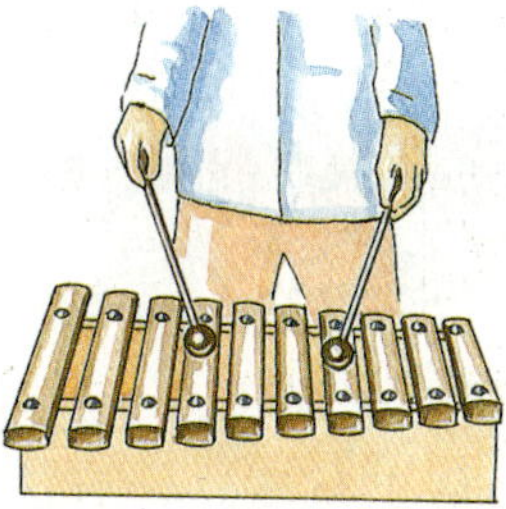

Y

yacht a small sailing boat used for pleasure or racing

yard an enclosed area of ground next to a building

DICTIONARY 191

Y

yarn 1. thread used for weaving
2. a long interesting story

yawn to draw in a long breath with one's mouth open

year the time taken for the Earth to go around the Sun once (365 days)

yell to cry out in a loud voice

yellow the colour of gold and sunshine

yelp a short, sharp bark of a dog in pain

yesterday the day before today

yew an evergreen tree with red berry-like cones

yield 1. to give way or surrender: *Ben yielded the fight to his opponent.*
2. to produce: *The tree yielded many nuts.*

yolk the yellow part of an egg

youth not old in years or existence; recently formed (young)

Z

zebra a wild animal like a horse with stripes on it's coat

zero nothing; the figure nought

zigzag a line with short, sharp turns

zip a fastener with metal or plastic interlocking teeth

zone an area of a particular climate

zoo a place where all sorts of animals are kept, studied and put on public display

192 DICTIONARY